To Greg & Melissa
on the third annual
Maine trek

Baird

Educational Myths
I Have Known and Loved

OTHER BOOKS BY THE AUTHOR

Don't Hold Them Back
John Hoskyns, Serjeant-at-Law
The Gospel
From These Beginnings

Educational Myths
I Have Known and Loved

BAIRD W. WHITLOCK

SCHOCKEN BOOKS · NEW YORK

First published by Schocken Books 1986
10 9 8 7 6 5 4 3 2 1   86 87 88 89
Copyright © 1986 by Baird W. Whitlock

Library of Congress Cataloging in Publication Data
Whitlock, Baird W.
Educational myths I have known and loved.
1. College teaching—United States—Addresses, essays,
lectures. 2. Universities and colleges—United States—
Addresses, essays, lectures. I. Title.
LB2331.72.W45 1986   378'.125'0973   84–27720

Design by Nancy Dale Muldoon
Manufactured in the United States of America
ISBN 0–8052–3989–8

Eight of these essays have appeared in the last two years in issues of the *International Quarterly*, a journal for teachers in international schools around the world.

Contents

Preface

ANY book of essays that takes stands of an argumentative nature based on personal experience ought, at the very least, to offer the reader a reason to believe that the experience has some validity. My decision to write about what I consider to be half-truths or even untruths in the field of education is based on thirty-five years of experience in college teaching. Since I started teaching at Middlebury College in 1948, I have taught at the University of Vermont, Colby College, Case Institute of Technology (now part of Case Western Reserve), San Francisco State College (now University), the University of Hawaii, the University of Wyoming, Elmira College, Simon's Rock, Philips Andover Academy, and Midwestern State University. That covers most of the United States, with the exception of the Northwest and the Southeast, but I have belonged to organizations that have brought me to conferences and discussions with faculty in those two regions as well.

During that period of time, of course, I have been everything from instructor through full professor and visiting lecturer; I have been chairman of four English departments, Dean of Humanities, Language, and Literature, and of Humanities and Social Sciences, and president of a small experimental college. I have taught in small coed colleges, a small male college and a small female college, and medium and large universities; in private institutions and state universities. The colleges have ranged in size from 200 students to 15,000. I have taught in nine English departments, six humanities programs, held a Chair of Music, and taught art history, philosophy, and courses in foreign film. My classes have ranged from a senior-high level Shakespeare seminar at Andover through graduate courses at four universities.

As for national and regional organizations, I have been a member of fifteen professional societies, an officer in four, and presented papers for eleven. I have also served on two college boards of trustees. I have received two major awards for teaching and three grants from foundations such as Ford and Carnegie. I have also been the Bildner Foundation Fellow and given a lecture series to Association of American Independent Schools in Brazil, Paraguay, Bolivia, and Chile. And I have been a consultant and evaluation visitor at seventeen colleges and universities for the Middle States Association and the New York State Education Department. Among the works that I have published on educational subjects is a book entitled *Don't Hold Them Back,* a discussion of early college programs in the United States, for the College Board.

None of this, of course, proves whether my opinions are correct or not, but it does at least show that they are based on a wide range of experience. I also hope it indicates that those opinions are worth paying attention to.

Ashburnham, Massachusetts

*Educational Myths
I Have Known and Loved*

That We Should Go Back to Basics

PERHAPS the best place to start an essay that claims to be a plea for reality in the teaching of composition is to state the author's credentials. I taught my first freshman English class at Middlebury College, Vermont, in the fall of 1948, and since then have taught composition at ten colleges and universities in all parts of the United States and in all kinds of institutions, including a fine private school. My students have ranged in age from fifteen to eighty-five years. On the basis of that experience I want to posit a controversial point: students from the same educational and family backgrounds are doing about the same kind of writing today, with the same kinds of errors, as in 1948 or any year in between. My major point, then, is that any argument for "Back to Basics" is flawed by the fact that the basics didn't work very well in the 40s and early 50s, which is the reason that teachers moved away from them (not during the late 60s, as it is often argued). To return to what didn't work in the first place is not a very logical or realistic procedure.

What, then, is the alternative? I would suggest that the cry should be, instead, "Forward to Fundamentals," for it remains true that all teachers of composition know that certain things are true. It is also true, however, that we usually do not act on the basis of our knowledge.

There is one piece of pedagogical knowledge that is shared by every teacher in the world. We all know it to be true. It is, simply, that the best way to learn is to teach. Yet almost no one of us utilizes that very basic piece of knowledge. There are lots of reasons for our failure. We are not sure how to implement it, for one thing. Many of us have experienced highly unsuccessful attempts on the part of our teachers to have students take over individual classes, and we do not want to foist that experience off on our own students. But the fact stands there, staring us in the face: the best way to learn *is* to teach. We also know that a great many of the experiments of the 60s worked well, especially the tutoring programs set up for college students among disadvantaged school children. I am not sure how much they helped the disadvantaged students but they certainly helped the tutors. Perhaps the assignment of upper division students as tutors to freshmen and sophomores might be one way of using our knowledge of the learning process instead of going to more upper division composition courses as some colleges are doing. Perhaps breaking up our classes into smaller groups, each of which is instructed by the students in the group on a rotating basis, might work. At any rate, we know the truth of the generalization. Probably *any* attempt to put it into practice would be beneficial.

Second, we all know that writing is a function secondary to speaking. That fact is echoed in the recent college text title *Writing Is an Unnatural Act.* Paul Goodman used to make the point that we are all lucky that we learned to speak without teachers, or otherwise we would probably all speak as poorly as we write. He had a point, although it was a narrow and selective one. But it is important to realize that all of us basically write what we "hear." The student who hears poor English is probably going to write it. I want to give two examples of methods that have an effect on writing styles (and spelling). The first is the case of a young instructor at Columbia University in the late 40s. The second is the case of a young woman I had in class during my first summer at Midwestern State University.

I believe that it was in 1948 that a young man was hired at Columbia and turned loose on his freshman sections. Soon the rest of the faculty discovered that something terribly subversive was going on in his classroom. None of his students were writing papers. Moreover, there was no homework. They were reading aloud in class. Each Friday, he ran a "Reading Bee" of increasingly more difficult selections. He once said, "I never was able to get through the 'Rime of the Ancient Mariner' with anyone still standing." He emphasized not only correct pronunciation but intelligent stressing of words and emphasis within phrases and clauses as signaled by the punctuation. Finally, just before Christmas (under the old college calendar), the students began to write. By the time of the finals in late January, his students were writing better themes than were those in the more traditional classes. His purpose had been for the students to "hear" good English before they started writing. The fact of the matter is that no one of us writes according to rule. We only think grammar when we are in trouble with a sentence. Usually we write with our ears leading the way. Yet most of us teach writing as a disembodied act or as a group of abstractions that we ourselves seldom or never use.

In my first summer at Midwestern, I assigned a number of oral reports in a sophomore literature course. One student, who had been silent up to the moment that it was her turn to take over the class, stood up and began a report in a voice that contained not the slightest hint of a Texas accent. That surprised me, as I had not known I had any Northerners in that section. After class I asked where she was from. In the broadest possible northern Texas accent, she answered, "Bowie." After the considerable initial shock—all too obvious, I am afraid—I asked why her report was so different from her normal speech. Her answer was that she had had a speech teacher in high school who would not let her students "talk Texan" when giving class reports. Interestingly enough, her papers for the class were not nearly as good as her oral reports. I suggested that for her next paper she use a tape recorder after working up an outline and try to present an oral report on the subject to herself, then type up the result. Her papers immediately improved markedly. She was "hearing" a different model for her writing.

It is an easy matter to implement our knowledge on this point. Having members of a class take turns reading aloud accomplishes a great deal—but only if they are not allowed to get away with mistakes. The best method in my experience is simply to say "No" after a sentence has been read with an error and ask the next person in line to read it. Soon the rest of the class members will become good judges of whether a sentence is read correctly or not. Occasionally, as with Dickens, the punctuation will not work in a particular sentence, making it impossible for the students to read it correctly. They will have learned a valuable lesson in proper punctuation. (There is an added advantage to this technique, incidentally: it is often easier to pick up problems of dyslexia this way than through analyzing errors in papers.) Some school teachers have told me that this practice is bad because it makes students feel self-conscious in class and may damage delicate psyches. In turn, I ask, "Is it better for a student to learn how to communicate properly and accurately in the relative friendliness of a classroom with a group of friends or to wait until his or her lack of skill leads to the loss of a job later on in life or leaves that student open to strangers' judgments of his stupidity?"

Third, writing *well* is a secondary function of reading. This is, of course, the experience of all creative writers. If we are honest with ourselves, it is our own experience as well. There has been a tendency recently to eliminate much of the reading of literature or good prose essays in the teaching of writing. But everyone needs the experience of reading good writing in order to find out how to better one's own style.

There is a second part to this piece of knowledge, again best stated in the form of a book title: *You Can't Write Writing*. It seems to me that one of the more horrible results of the recent emphasis on rhetoric is the tendency to spend all the time in class talking about writing. But writing can only occur when someone has something to say. Obviously students can talk about their own experiences, but that can be deadening to both student and teacher after a while. Reading good literature automatically provides subject matter about which to write. I emphasize the adjective "good" because there has also been a tendency, it seems to me, in recent anthologies to include work that simply isn't particularly good writing. Students have enough poor models to work from in their lives without having the number increased by class assignments.

Fourth, correct spelling comes either from proper speaking or from reading. This is another way of emphasizing the need for the twofold approach of phonetics and sight spelling. In Texas, for example, my experience has been that the attack on spelling has to be twofold. Many students simply are not aware that when they write "pin" for "pen" they are doing a very natural act, for that is how they say the word. Unless a good deal of time can be spent on proper speaking, substantial reading (with a dictionary at hand) is an absolute necessity.

Fifth, and perhaps most important, the only way to learn to write is to write. Robert Frost used to say that it is far more important that the student write than that the teacher correct what he or she writes. As a matter of fact, if most of us are honest with ourselves, we know that most students look only at the grade the teacher puts at the beginning or end of the paper, even though we have made all kinds of inked or penciled comments in the margins.

The most important experiment in the teaching of writing of which I am aware took place at San Jose State College while I was department chairman at San Francisco State in the early 60s. For three years, a program was run in which every teacher taught two different sections of composition. In one section, the teacher used a rhetoric and handbook, taught grammar, assigned themes, held conferences, and all those other good things that we take to be self-evident. In the other section, the teacher simply told the students to write for fifty minutes each class. Attendance was compulsory, and the students had to write all the time, even if it were only to put down x's. You can imagine how boring writing "x x x x x x" becomes after a while. Papers were not handed back. Students could come in for conferences, but they didn't. The teacher made charts on all students, noting the number of misspellings, punctuation mistakes, faulty references, and so on. The results were astounding. Spelling cleared up first, then punctuation, then grammar faults. Naturally, the level of usage did not change much. At the end of the semester, all students were given the same exam, which consisted of a section of short-answer questions on grammar and usage and a longer section on an assigned theme. In every semester of the experiment, there was a clear and verifiable difference between the class sections. The students in the free writing sections did better than those in the standard courses. I know of no experiment in the teaching of composition that was handled more tightly or had such clear evidence of what we all know to be basic about learning how to write.

Every year that I teach composition, I try some form of this experiment, usually having free writing for the first ten or fifteen minutes of the class. The same results occur every time. The rationale is clear enough. Almost all students have been taught grammar at one time or another and its rules are in the synaptic connections of their brains, whether the students are aware of it or not. And, after all, no student purposely misspells words, especially words that he has seen at one time or another. The free writing practice does away with the inhibitory factors that keep the student from utilizing the knowledge that he or she actually possesses in the brain.

There is another lesson here. Everyone knows that a teacher can only correct so many papers during a semester. But it is more important that the students write than that the teacher correct all that is written. If a teacher makes clear that not all papers will be corrected but gives the number that will be, students will accept that. If they want to gamble on which ones are corrected, that is up to them. Obviously, all final papers have to be corrected.

Sixth, we all know that traditional grammar rules are

neither absolute nor complete. Try to explain what part of speech "swimming" is in the sentence "I am going swimming."! But most of us find that traditional grammar rules are a lot more helpful to students than are any of the more recent variations. It seems to me that a combination of traditional grammar with an emphasis on the structure of sentences makes the best sense. That is why I still find using diagrams on a blackboard a helpful way of teaching about problems of grammar. It can also be fun if you throw a good page-and-a-half sentence of Samuel Johnson's at them, as my ninth-grade teacher did to us. It also provides a tool for them to use when they get stuck in their own sentences. And it also helps students to see why a sentence is easier to read and construe when modifiers are placed next to the word they modify.

It has always seemed important to me for English teachers to admit that we honestly don't know how to teach writing. If anyone had the answer to that one, he or she could become a millionaire overnight. Most of us do know how to correct or edit, however, and that is what we are really doing when we say we are teaching writing. This would seem to imply that we *can* teach them what we do well, and that is the point at which revising and editing comes in. Too often we have students write papers which we edit, and, like a one-night high school play, the fun is over before the chance for a really good performance is possible. I suspect that one of the problems on this point is that many teachers do not themselves really rewrite. We write, correct, and retype. But we seldom even require that much from our students.

There is a famous story of William James, who was approached after a lecture one night by a lady who asked him his opinion on a certain subject. James immediately replied, "I don't know; I haven't said anything yet." There are very few people in this world who really think to themselves. Perhaps it takes a saint or philosopher. Most of us deal in reverie of one sort or another. Even our most serious attempts to think about a subject tend to wander off into fantasy. There are two times at which we really discover what we think: when we speak and when we write. The advantage of the second is that we are forced to think even more clearly, precisely, and, we trust, coherently. This point can be made to students and can be made forcefully because the teacher can identify with the fact itself. If we cannot write clearly, it is probably true, as Montaigne pointed out centuries ago, that we probably are not thinking clearly. If we fail to communicate clearly, it is likely that we do not know clearly what it is we wish to communicate.

The first step in good teaching ought to be honesty. It is important for teachers of composition to be honest about what we know and what we do not know. My suggestion of moving forward to fundamentals is to discover just what it is that we do know about writing and start from there. Otherwise, we will speak positively about a number of things we consider self-evident and fall under the eternal judgment of Ambrose Bierce's definitions: self-evident—"evident to oneself and to no one else," and positive—"being wrong at the top of one's voice."

That Memory Counts in America

BESIDES the basic moral errors which Richard Nixon made during the Watergate days, he made an even greater blunder. It is strange that he did so, as he should have known the political climate of America better than that. What he should have done is tell the truth about the tapes, and about Watergate, and then go right on being president. The fact is that the American people would have forgotten very quickly. They always do. As a group, we probably have the shortest memory of any nation in the history of mankind. There are all kinds of evidence to support that claim.

Take Mr. Nixon, for example. His own California campaigns had been forgotten when he ran for President. Back in the late 40s he had conducted one of the vilest campaigns, against Helen Gahagan Douglas, that California had ever seen. Most people in the country knew about the falsified photographs of Douglas and the head of the Communist Party, Gus Hall. Nixon at that point knew what he was doing. He simply said that he was sorry that the photograph had been published but that he himself had not done anything wrong. The photograph continued to be circulated, and Mr. Nixon won. When he ran for Governor of California, and lost—promising that we would not have to put up with him any more and failing to keep even that promise, as he knew that no one would pay any attention to it—he committed all of the dirty tricks that characterized Watergate later on, and he and his cohorts were actually convicted in court of those dirty tricks. Americans forgot.

But it is not only Richard Nixon whose evil deeds have

been forgotten. Take President Lyndon Johnson for another example. I suspect that most Americans do not even remember the Dominican Republic crisis. During our invasion of the Dominican Republic, President Johnson issued absolutely conflicting statements of what was happening about every six hours. And all the newspaper, television, and radio commentators took for granted that each time the president was telling the truth, when actually he was simply making up a new story. No one remembered. He was almost as bad about Vietnam, as we all know now, and as most of us really knew then. What frightens me is that it now looks as if the American people are being treated to "scholarly" revisions on Vietnam that will erase everything we knew was going wrong while we were involved. It should all make for good reading on Central America some day.

There are educational implications to this lack of memory, unfortunately. American education keeps reinventing the wheel. For example, I have been involved in setting up interdisciplinary programs at various colleges ever since 1953, when I began the Humanities Program at Colby College in Maine. I believe in interdisciplinary studies very deeply, and I have helped to set up five such programs at other colleges since then. But the interesting thing to me is that about every ten years someone comes along and discovers that we really ought to go the route of interdisciplinary studies. This discovery is always made with the shock of the new. We then have conferences on how we ought to go about having interdisciplinary studies. Bright young people come in and tell about what they plan to do in the next year or two, or what they have done in their first year of implementing a program. No one goes back and asks anyone who has been working in the humanities for years what happened before. As a result, all the same mistakes are made, and, luckily, the same benefits are discovered, if much too slowly.

At the moment of this writing, the President of the United States is wandering around the country calling for Back to

Basics. Why? As I have said in the previous essay, the basics didn't work before. Not only were they badly taught, but they were often based on untrue theses. English grammar does not work the way Latin grammar does. Two and two equal four only in those circumstances in which the mathematician sets up that configuration of numbers. As a matter of fact, two plus two in computer work equals twenty-two. I am sorry to say that the best "humanities" course I ever encountered was a freshman mathematics course at Case Institute, in which, for the first few weeks, each instructor began each class period with the question "What does two plus two equal?" and then, when given some strange answer like "273" would proceed to work out a perfectly justifiable—usually quite practical as well—system in which two plus two equals 273. It made the students question the assumptions with which they grew up and made them think afresh about what they considered "basic" truths.

One of the most misjudged educational ventures of my lifetime was the New Math. New Math was based on absolutely sound mathematical knowledge and teaching approaches. My own son was doing algebra problems in first grade. When we moved away from Cleveland, Ohio, he went backward mathematically and did not reach the same stage of mathematical comprehension that he had gained in first grade until he reached tenth grade. Why then was New Math dropped, and why did it come under such criticism? One answer is that it too forgot the past. The only problem with New Math was that teachers neglected at the same time to provide students with the necessary tools to do computation. It was a perfectly good idea to teach set theory at the very beginning of a student's mathematical knowledge, but that did not mean that the student did not need to learn the three-times table in the third grade. (And we seem to be forgetting the same lesson when we provide calculators and computers for young students today! I saw a young girl at a check-out counter the other day fall apart in absolute panic when the battery of her hand calculator began to run out. She admitted that she wasn't sure that she could add a column of figures in her head.) There was, of course, an even deeper reason for the failure of New Math, unfortunately. It was the fact that the teachers were not as able as the students to grasp the new approach to mathematics. The blame here should be placed squarely on education department requirements in colleges and universities across the United States. I know of no education program that requires of the education major the same level of mathematical ability as is required of the ordinary student in either the liberal arts or sciences. This is a disgraceful situation, and one that will never be changed as long as education programs are left to educationists.

The history of American education is a constant wandering back and forth between allowing a choice of electives and requiring a general education for any specific group of students. At the moment we are on the side of requirements. This is particularly true within specific departmental majors. Most majors are now stealing almost every possible hour from their students, so that it is often impossible for a student to get a good education. This pendulum swing between electives and requirements in American education is probably not something that is going to stop, nor would it necessarily be a good thing if it did. But surely, each time the swing occurs, we can do without the nonsense of having educators and newspaper reporters acting as if something really new were happening.

One of the real problems with changes in American education is that faculties never really give any new program a chance to survive. They vote in the new program, and then even before it has a chance to prove itself, they begin to make changes in it. They never do test whether the program will work or not. There probably ought to be a rule like that which used to hold in the Polish Parliament in earlier centuries. When a law was passed in Poland, it could not be changed until the man who brought up the law voted to change it. Therefore, anyone who wanted his law to remain in effect any length of time simply got on his horse immediately after the vote and rode out of the country. Solon pulled the same trick on the people of Athens. He agreed to draw up a set of laws for the city if he would be the only person who could change those laws for ten years; then he traveled for ten years so that no one could force him to change them. Perhaps what is needed is a rule stating that when a new program is instituted, it cannot be changed for at least five years.

But there may be an even deeper lesson for American education to be learned from all this, one about which almost no one agrees with me. It goes back to an argument that is as old as philosophy, but best expressed by Edmund Spenser in the Mutability Cantos. In these cantos, the argument is that unless there is some unchangeable law in the universe, one cannot believe there is a God. And yet everywhere one looks, there is mutability or change, the change in plants, the change in seasons, the change in people. But the cantos come to an end with a remarkable conclusion. There is a constant in the universe, the constant of change. Therefore God does exist.

Perhaps that would be the best answer for American education. I believe that there is a virtue in change for its own sake. But most educators will insist, when they propose a new program, that they believe in this one specific change, but not in change for its own sake. There is much to be said for changes for their own sake. The famous Hawthorne Experiment proved that you could increase worker productivity simply by changing the physical environment. Almost every educational experiment has proved that you can motivate students to do a better job if you can convince them that they are part of an experimental program or section. Probably to get the best results in American education, we ought to put every student into an experimental section for the rest of his or her schooling. But that would require almost constant change, more than most teachers are up to.

But we can learn from past experience. We can remember those elements from the past that work, and as we keep changing our programs, we can reintroduce those elements from the past that have yielded the best results. Anyone for a section of New Math?

C

That Television Is Responsible for the Decline in SAT Scores

AS stated in the previous essay, while I was writing this book, the President of the United States was touring the country extolling the virtues of Back to Basics. Near the end of his trip, he repeatedly remarked that during the next ten years he hoped that we not only could halt the decline in SAT scores, but that we would see a return of those scores to the levels of the early 1960s, before they started to decline. There is, of course, an easy way to achieve that goal: first, permit only the same mix of students from the same schools that took the exams in the late 50s and early 60s to take them now; and second, increase the morale of the country.

Obviously the president does not know what he is talking about, but that should not surprise anyone. He has many models to follow of those who talk about College Board scores without understanding what their purpose is or what they accomplish. In 1977, when everyone in the country seemed to be going through the usual panic about the decline in Board scores, I was asked to make comments on the report of the panel that was set up by the College Board to examine the causes of the decline in SAT scores. I had recently been the president of an experimental college whose students were all one or two years younger than the usual college age, and I was currently writing a book, *Don't Hold Them Back,* under the auspices of the Ford Foundation and Carnegie Corporation, for the College Board, arguing the rationale for early college experience. As a result, I was deeply involved in such

programs as the Advanced Placement Program of the College Board. Lacking any control group with which to make
comparisons, the panel had been forced to come up with such
observations as the fact that students were watching more
and more television instead of reading books. The panel did
give lip service to the fact that one of the reasons for the
decline was the change in the group of students who were
taking the exam, but they certainly did not emphasize that
change as strongly as they should have. There were socio-
logical and political reasons for not doing so. They were
right in noting, however, that there was a decline among the
better, more traditional college-bound students as well.

College Board scores became an important measure for
judgments about entering college freshmen almost as soon
as the SAT exams became widely used in the late 1940s.
From that time on the average and mean scores on the
exams went up consistently and increased even more sharply
after the Sputnik crisis in the 1950s. They reached a high in
the spring of 1963, during Kennedy's term of office. In the
spring of 1964, following Kennedy's assassination, SAT
scores dropped sharply, and have continued to decline ever
since. One measure of the extent of the decline is that in the
late 60s, when I was screening students for the Liberal
Studies Program at Elmira College, I was actually able to
judge that students scoring lower than 430 on the SATs
would not be able to succeed in the program. If that were
still the measure for entrance admissions, most colleges
would be in very rough shape indeed.

A study of the declining scores on SATs does reveal some
interesting and important facts, however. It reveals the influence of public and national morale on education and on educational motivation. I suggest that it shows absolutely nothing about the influence of television.

In the first place, the major reason for the decline in SAT
scores is the fact that far greater numbers of students, of all
ranges of ability and backgrounds, are now taking the SAT
exams, rather than merely the college-bound students from

leading high schools and prep schools. That continuing change of the mix of students, students who are in many ways unlike the students who took the exams in the 50s, students who more and more are from nontraditional, non-college-bound backgrounds, is still at work and is a continuing reason for the decline in SAT scores. No one should be surprised by this, nor should anyone particularly panic about it. It is simply a fact of educational life. It is probably a good thing, as a matter of fact, as it indicates that more and more students are at least thinking about going to college than in the past.

But there is more than simply the overall decline in the scores to pay attention to. As one studies the graph of SAT scores, one finds that along with the general decline, there are specific drops or breaks downward that are in many cases quite remarkable, and, together, account for a major part of the overall decline in average scores. As I mentioned earlier, the first decline in SAT scores came in the semester following the assassination of John Fitzgerald Kennedy. The morale of the country was very low, and that low morale showed up in the scores achieved by the same type of students who had been taking the exams during the previous decade. Once one makes that first observation, the sharp breaks in the rest of the graph become remarkably clear. The next big break (following a partial recovery in 1967 after Johnson's reelection) in SAT scores comes in the exams taken just after the death of Martin Luther King and the shooting of Bobby Kennedy. During the next few years, the general decline sharpens, at the same time as disillusionment over the Vietnam War increased.

There are also positive movements in the graph of SAT scores, and no one pays any more than momentary heed to them. For example, there was a leveling off of the scores for the exams taken in the spring following Nixon's election, but by the next fall the decline once again began and sharpened during the Watergate period. After Carter's election there was a similar leveling off, followed by the continued decline,

only this time the decline was not as sharp, as the disenchant-
ment with Carter did not equal the public dismay following
Watergate. In the spring following Reagan's election there
was an actual increase in the Board scores, but, once again,
the general decline set in. During the election campaign in the
spring and fall of 1984, the scores again climbed.

There seems to me, as it did in 1977, to be a rather obvious
lesson to be drawn from studying the decline of SAT scores.
That is, that when we give students some reason for hope for
the future and for their country, SAT scores go up. There is
every reason to believe that if we were to find a way to give
high school seniors some genuine hope for their futures, we
could at least halt the decline in Board scores and perhaps
even bring about a slight rise, although that rise would never
be very great as long as the mix of students taking the exams
remains as varied as it is.

But there is something wrong with this entire discussion,
and educators and politicians alike should be ashamed of
themselves for continuing to misuse SAT scores. In the first
place, no one talks about the fact that as SAT scores decrease,
other indicators show that high school seniors today have far
more "knowledge" at their fingertips than preceding genera-
tions of students. There simply is more to know and more to
learn than there used to be. Whether it is more important or
not is a different question. In the second place, SAT exams
were not designed to provide information for generalized
statements about the state of American education or the ability of groups of graduating high school seniors. The College
Board has always defined the SATs in a very clear and precise
way: it has said that the SAT scores, taken in conjunction
with the student's high school record, is the best indicator of
a student's performance during the freshman year in college.
That is all the College Board has ever claimed. It is an indicator of an individual student's performance in his first year in
college. It is nothing else. SATs were not established as examinations that would reveal any generalized data about high

school education. They were set up as an indicator of an individual student and his or her ability to succeed in college.

If we want to worry about parts of our educational program, or if we want to change the present situation, there are relatively easy ways of going about it. For example, if what we really mean when we complain about SAT scores is that students cannot write or that they cannot do mathematical problems, then there are practical solutions. We can make students write more in high school, and we can require more mathematics courses, taken to a higher level. I suspect that in the case of mathematics, it also means that we must get better teachers of mathematics or that we must require our future teachers to take better mathematics courses in college.

But all of us would benefit greatly, and there would be increased clarity in our discussions about education, if we would stop using the SAT scores as a measure of anything except what they were established to measure: the performance of an individual student, at an individual college, in his or her first year.

D

That You Can Teach How to Teach

IN 1970, while I was teaching at Elmira College, I was named one of the ten Master Teachers in the State of New York by someone in Albany—the basis for which I knew nothing then and still know nothing. The idea was that we were to go to Hamilton College during the summer for a week and meet with some hundred-plus new college teachers. They didn't have to be young, but they had to be within the first three years of their college teaching experience. The idea implied in the letter I received was that we were to teach them how to teach. My immediate reaction was a simple one. I wrote back that I didn't believe you could teach anyone how to teach, but thank you very much for asking.

During the next twenty-four hours I thought about it a little more carefully. I realized that there was a chance that they were going to get ten people from somewhere who would go to Hamilton and try to tell a hundred perfectly good young teachers how they ought to teach. I called Albany the following day and said I had changed my mind, and I gratefully accepted the charge.

When I arrived at Hamilton I began talking with the other faculty members who had been selected and found to my great relief that eight out of the nine had initially turned down the offer and then changed their minds for exactly the same reasons that I did. I regretfully must record that one of the ten did arrive at Hamilton planning to tell the teachers how to teach. He was an apparently well-known instructor at the Fashion Institute in New York. In later years I also discovered more about many of the college staff in the State Board offices and came to realize that they had hoped we would take the position we took.

During the next few days we had some very boring planned programs during the day, followed by some marvelous late afternoon and evening informal sessions in rooms around the dormitories. The set meetings suffered from the fact that there isn't really very much you can say about teaching in general unless you are interested in gimmicks, and gimmicks only work for those to whom they come naturally. But there are all kinds of bases for discussions about teaching among those who have faced actual classroom problems and found solutions for the individual situations in which they have found themselves; teachers want to know if the solutions they have found workable make sense to anyone else.

Somewhere along the way that week each person shared some personal conviction that he or she held deeply, but convictions like that don't come out easily. It is usually one or two in the morning before they begin to. My own conviction runs something like this: no one is ever going to solve the basic problem of whether you teach people or subject matter; I think it is really a silly conflict. I doubt if you ever want to teach anybody anything unless you love the subject itself; and unless you like the people you are teaching, the love for the subject matter itself isn't going to do anybody any good. But I am sure that the inherent nature of the teaching situation involves people at an emotional level, and I don't hesitate to say that it is a sexual level.

Teachers are parent figures whether they want to be or not. Age makes no difference whatever. I learned that early, when I walked into my first college classroom as a teacher three months after graduating from undergraduate work myself. I have had students as old as eighty-five in class, and it was true with the oldest student I ever had that I became her "father" in a very basic way. Because this is true, the teacher who violates the emotional/sexual relationship is doing a major injury to the student involved. Questions of whether a student is old enough to make decisions about emotional involvement, and so on, are beside the point. The main point is that the teaching relationship is a parent/child relationship at its heart, and no teacher ought to violate that. I know that during the 60s (and since that time), teachers, especially college teachers, have tried to argue that they are not parent figures and that they are somehow or other colearners with their students. But the very teachers whom I have seen and heard arguing that way are the ones who most often violate the student-teacher relationship for their own benefit.

What I said one night to a group of young teachers at Hamilton I still feel deeply: any faculty member who does not recognize the sexual nature of the relationship between students and faculty members is either stupid or too repressed to handle reality very easily. Any good teacher is going to acknowledge that relationship and probably play on it in one way or another, at least certainly accept it as being true. But any teacher who lets that relationship turn into an overtly sexual one is violating that student and the nature of the whole teacher-student relationship—almost in an incestuous way—and ultimately is harming that student emotionally and intellectually because of the mixing up of the various aspects of the teacher-student relationship.

Now what does all this have to do with the question of whether you can or cannot teach anyone how to teach? A very great deal. It means that the heart of the relationship between teacher and student is twofold. The first is the subject matter. Taking courses in education rather than in subject matter is probably the most wasteful thing a college student can do. I say that without the slightest hesitation. But at the same time, the subject matter has to be communicated, and the question is how do you learn to communicate it? Ultimately, I suggest, it is communicated by love, and in the case of teaching, it is love of the student *and* of the subject matter. You can't teach love. You can't teach caring. You can say, for example, that it is a good thing to learn the first names—or at least the names—of each of the students in your classes. This is true. There is no question that students at any age react very well to being known by name. We all do. We all like that personal touch. But if a person really doesn't like students—and there are a great many teachers, unfortunately, who don't—the fact that the teacher knows their names will not make the students feel any better about being in class. In that case learning first names is merely a gimmick.

Throughout the history of literature, and of art in general, there is a generalization that holds true with such validity that I doubt if any of us would question that there is at least a grain of truth in it: children and animals have a unique sense of what a person is really like. Dogs veer away from persons whom they seem to sense dislike them. Children do not believe their parents when the latter tell them that "so-and-so is coming for a visit and really likes kids," when the children know better. If it is true that children sense what adults really feel or are really like, despite their outward statements (or even actions), then any method taught in education classes about communicating caring or affection is bound to fail because children or young adults are going to know if and when it is false.

In third grade we had a young teacher who was terribly cute—we all knew it even in third grade. She was very nice, she was very inexperienced, and we picked on her a great deal. She really didn't know how to handle us, and I suppose one could argue that if she had had the right kind of education course, she might have learned how to handle us. I doubt if that is true. Most of what is communicated in education courses is boredom, and it is not by boredom that a third-grade teacher is going to communicate with a group of third-graders. We were being particularly obnoxious at one point while we were learning the three-times table. I think

Peter Lufburrow was throwing things at Alfred Paul; maybe George Leonard and I were just talking loudly with each other when we shouldn't have been. I doubt if it was one of the girls; they tended to be terribly "nice" in third grade. At any rate, the teacher tried hitting the blackboard a couple of times and clapping her hands (if she had been able to clap her hands the way our seventh-grade teacher did, she would have had us all cowed anyway). Nothing worked. Finally, she excused herself for a minute and went into the cloakroom that ran all along one side of our classroom. It had two doors that allowed for continuous motion of young people grabbing coats and overshoes on the way into and out of school. At one end of it there was a small window facing a miniature courtyard or airshaft. Being nasty little third-graders, we decided we would find out what she was doing in the cloakroom, so several of us tiptoed quietly to the door she had *not* gone through. We opened it stealthily and peeked through. At the other end of the cloakroom, silhouetted against the window, stood our young teacher, handkerchief to eyes, crying her young heart out. We closed the door—very carefully. From that moment on, and for the rest of the year—certainly at least until the twelve-times table—if she had asked us to jump into the Raritan River or walk down to the Atlantic Ocean and try wading to Europe, we would have done it without hesitation.

What would the educationists have us do? Teach new teachers to go into the cloakroom and cry when their students pick on them? The answer, of course, is that you can't teach the answer to a situation of that kind. All a teacher can do is react honestly. I am not saying that there are no techniques that can be taught, especially in the lower grades. I do not know what they are, but I am sure they are learned better by having a group of teachers sit around talking with each other than they are in a college classroom situation with a college professor instructing future teachers how to teach kindergarten children.

I am convinced that any group of education courses that

takes away from the opportunity for future teachers to engage in a good, broad range of academic courses does abiding harm to those who are going into teaching. I do know for certain that the large body of education requirements keeps a great number of excellent potential teachers from considering education as a vocation, and that is criminal.

That Newspapers Are Up-to-Date on Education

HERMANN Hesse, near the beginning of his novel *The Glass Bead Game,* describes the modern age as the age of feuilletonism, an age filled with gossip and chitchat instead of real information and ideas. One needs no better example of his point than any morning television talk show, on which all the latest fads and ill-considered nonsense are reported and discussed with equal seriousness, no matter how silly or unscientific they may be. Opinion, not reason, runs rampant.

I first became aware of how out-of-date—and therefore incorrect—newspapers were in their treatment of education, and how disconnected from the real world of the college campus they were, when, in the fall of 1970, I noticed that newspapers across the country were discussing the college and university climate as if it were still the previous school year; but, of course, everything had changed. As a matter of fact, it took the newspapers more than a year to catch up with the change, the same period of time that it usually takes newspapers to find out what is actually happening in education. This hiatus between events and their being reported sometimes has unfortunate consequences. For example, the current discussion of the decline of educational standards and training almost always neglects the evidence that almost every study in recent years has shown: that students through at least the fourth grade and in some cases up through the seventh grade are doing better than their predecessors in the previous decade. And each year that improvement advances one grade. A turn-about has been accomplished, but newspapers are not paying attention to it. They are paying attention only to the high school juniors and seniors, who take the SATs. I have never in my lifetime read a really good newspaper article on the SATs. Not one has emphasized the true purpose of those exams.

There are several reasons for such mismanagement of news. The first is that reporters often insert their own experience into the current educational situation, a human failing and quite understandable, but also very misleading. Not only is their experience already out of date, but memories of one's own education are often among the more inaccurate items of the human mind. As I listen to some of my former students discuss their college educations, I am amazed to hear statements that relate only marginally to what I know happened to them or was going on at that college at the time.

Elsewhere in this collection I tell of returning to my high school after years of teaching and having a long talk with former classmates. Several of them expressed their opinions about what a good education we had received and what good teachers we had. I demurred on the second point and suggested that we really had only one good teacher. When my friends seemed surprised, I went through the list, citing details of incompetence, poor training, or just plain laziness. One person then said, "You're right, but in that case, how come we got such a good education?" My answer was brief: "They all shared one great characteristic. They never got in our way. They let us learn on our own and from each other." And in every case I could give an example, such as the English teacher who never corrected a theme (we ran several specific checks on that), but let us read and act out Shakespeare and discuss the plays on our own.

In the second place, newspaper reporters tend to listen almost entirely to people in places of authority or to malcontents. The former are anxious to show that everything is just fine, and the latter are just as anxious to show that nothing is right. Part of the reason for the reporters' choices is that they want a good "news" story rather than to find out what the truth is. But there is a further element: they tend to listen to the "experts." In stories on education, this means that they listen to educationists, and educationists are more a part of the problem itself than they are a source of information about the situation or any possible solutions to existing problems. There is still another difficulty. Even when reporters do their homework well, they tend to lean on published works that are already accepted in the field. Now the problem with that approach is simply that these works are already one to four years out of date. That is the nature of the publishing business. It takes a year at least for a reputable book on education to be written. It then takes another year for the publisher to get the book off the press, and it probably takes another year for the book to have a circulation wide enough for people to react intelligently to it.

This matter of the time period that elapses before any newspaper article on a given subject matter appears is important. Anyone who is used to teaching college freshman classes knows that every entering class is different, both from the one preceding it and the one following it. (There was an exception to this rule in the last two or three years of the 1960s, when high school students were aping their college friends and relatives.) Strangely enough, as I have indicated elsewhere, students in any given year are very much the same in all parts of the country. But to make judgments on a given class or year on the basis of the previous class or year is to be misled and misleading.

And, finally, the reporting is inaccurate because of one of the basic problems of the journalistic profession. For whatever reasons, and I suspect that the main reason is the sheer pressure of time, there is usually no long-term research done on educational problems for newspaper articles. The result is that every time a newspaper reporter reports on a subject, he acts as if it were something new in the world. If he cannot treat it as an immediate news item, he is not interested. The result is that programs that have been under way for years are always treated as if they are brand new programs or experiments that no one has ever heard of or that no one is quite sure of. I know that is true of a college like Simon's Rock, whose student body, made up of students entering after tenth or eleventh grade, is constantly a source of amazement to newspaper reporters. The reporters, therefore, in their articles, always write as if Simon's Rock had come into existence the day before yesterday, rather than being a college that has operated with very high standards and with magnificent results for the past twenty years.

There is no solution to the problem, as the journalistic profession will undoubtedly remain what it currently is, but there is one particularly difficult result of the problem. Newspapers are very much alike, which means that it is difficult to find out whether a particular article is up-to-date, out-of-date, or whatever, for all of the newspapers will be following much the same fads in much the same way. My only suggestion is that one read all articles on education with several pounds of salt at hand. I also suggest that any one interested in what is going on in education should talk to someone in teaching at the moment, or talk to students who are in the classrooms. But newspaper people are certainly not the ones to talk to or listen to about what is going on.

What is so strange to me, and always has been, is the number of teachers who accept newspaper reports as to what is happening. As a result, they often find themselves deep in depression when the newspaper writers tell them they ought to be, whereas actually they are probably having a pretty good time in the classroom, working with some remarkably good students. Such teachers should stop reading the newspapers or stick to the comic pages.

That One Educational Method Is Better than Another

WHEN I began teaching, I was lucky enough to land a job at Middlebury College right after my senior year. The college was small, it was coed, and all the classes were small enough to permit discussion rather than requiring lectures. By the end of three years I was thoroughly convinced that this was the only way that a good college education could take place. Then I went to the University of Edinburgh in Scotland for graduate work. Here all the classes were large, the lecture method was universal, and when a professor did allow a chance for discussion, the students steadfastly refused to accept the bait. It was also obvious, of course, that these students were getting an excellent education. There must have been something wrong with my generalization.

Since that time I have been a part of all kinds of institutions and watched all kinds of teachers; and I have been placed in all kinds of teaching situations myself, from tutorial to large lecture. In the Liberal Studies Program at Elmira College, we even set up a situation in which the teacher was occasionally supposed to be a colearner with his students. It worked.

One of the ways of testing the generalization that one educational method is better than another is to think back to one's own really good or great teachers. I think most of us as teachers would prefer a classroom situation in which as much discussion as possible takes place. It makes "good educational sense." The fact is, however, that most of us have memories of great teachers who were, almost without exception, great lecturers rather than discussion leaders. (I am not including graduate seminars in this consideration; that is a different ball of wax, or can of worms, depending on one's experience.)

There are some practical lessons to be learned by recognizing that all kinds of educational or teaching methods work (or do not work, depending on the context). The first is one that faculty members in general do not wish to face. That is, if a teacher lectures, it makes no difference whatever what size the class is in front of that teacher. (Class size *does*, however, make a very large difference in what kind of writing or testing can be used.) I know many teachers who would fight to the death for classes of fifteen to twenty, and yet they themselves lecture 90 per cent of the time. Once I found out that you could learn in classes of all sizes, I was less hesitant to take on lecture-size classes. In the process I discovered, first in a class on the English novel with fifty students, and then in a film class of ninety-five, that you can have some of the best discussions with a class whose size is generally considered too large for discussion. It takes more work on the part of the teacher, but the results can be magnificent. On the other hand, I have often discovered that some seminar classes are too small to allow for the mixture of opinions that are essential for the seminar set-up. It is important for a seminar student to listen to the ideas of his peers rather than to listen just to the teacher. If the ideas within the small group are not really different, the result is stultifying.

My favorite definition of the ideal student-teacher relationship is the old one of the teacher at one end of a log and the student at the other, and it is true that I have spent many wonderful hours and years working in tutorial situations. But the nature of the subject matter must be quite specific for the tutorial format to be better than a regular class. If the tutorial attempts to cover a wide range of reading, for example, there is a built-in block against the teacher giving enough background material to cover the breadth of material. It simply seems ridiculous to sit facing a single student and launch into a description of what the seventeenth century was like, for instance. On the other hand, working in detail on a single writer can be extremely beneficial in a tutorial. And there is one unmixed blessing to the tutorial: it gives the student, indeed demands of the student, more practice in writing and speaking his or her own ideas than does the normal classroom situation.

I think one of the more interesting requirements in American educational history is one that Sarah Lawrence used to state in its catalog. Sarah Lawrence, of course, has always been known for its individual instruction. But the requirement was that the student take at least one lecture course each year. That is a real switch from the usual American approach.

What is the answer then, if there is no better or best teaching method? Probably it is that a student should experience a variety of course approaches; but there is no rule for that either. Certainly there is no rule for the teacher of those courses. The best method for any individual teacher is what comes naturally. It is certainly true that to force on a teacher a teaching method that does not come naturally leads to some genuinely abominable classroom teaching. There are many teachers who simply can not lead a discussion. There are others who find it extremely difficult to give interesting and valuable lectures. Required class sizes of any kind, therefore, without attention being paid to the nature of the teachers involved, are not only misguided but often dangerous educational practice.

Perhaps what we need somewhere along the line are courses in *learning* methods, taught quite early in a student's experience. The student may discover what is his or her own best method of learning. In college that might pay off in ability to choose courses somewhat by the methods used by the teachers. But any generalization is dangerous, and this suggestion is as dangerous as any. It implies something of the sort of thing that is covered by the phrase "study habits." I have often wondered whose study habits we are talking about. Every student learns in a different way, or at least in a slightly different way. Adults are often appalled by the noise that surrounds their children when they study these days. As one who grew up with a radio playing while I was studying, I cannot really agree with their fears. If anyone suggested that I should study with a blank wall or clear desk in front of me, I could only respond that I cannot do that, and I am happy that no one ever tried to make me do it. Give me a window with a view any time. It helps me free my mind and let it wander. Better yet, let there be a mountain that I can throw my mind up against.

That Teachers Can Motivate Students

O NE of the major student complaints about teachers is that some do not motivate the students in their classes. I doubt if a teacher *can* motivate a student even if he tries. A good friend of mine who is an excellent and much-loved teacher used to go around quoting the statement that you can lead a student to a subject, but you can't make him think.

All too often both students and teachers mix up the terms "motivation" and "entertainment." There is a major difference between the two. Over the years, I have had to read literally thousands of student evaluations of faculty members in my departments. One of the problems in evaluating the evaluations is how to know what a student means when he says that a teacher is a "good" teacher. There is unfortunately no question but that this often means little more than that the teacher is entertaining. Luckily, with English teachers there is a relatively easy way to check whether the teacher is a good teacher or not. If the students doing the evaluation are unable to express themselves in decent English, then one has real reason to question whether the teacher is a good teacher rather than merely an entertaining one.

Many years ago I was honored by my old high school by being named Graduate of the Year. I never was sure what that meant, but I'm proud of my high school. When most of the high schools in the state of New Jersey were looking for things like basketball festivals to sponsor, my school sponsored a Shakespeare festival. I went back and gave a lecture on Shakespeare to the entire student body. In the afternoon, a group of my alumni friends and I sat around and, as is usually

the case, talked about our old teachers. We all agreed on who
our best teacher was. It was the Latin teacher, Miss Filene.
The reason that we all thought she was the best teacher was
summed up in a phrase used by all of us in exactly the same
words: "She made us work."

I do not remember a single thing that Miss Filene did to
"motivate" us. It is true that she occasionally tried to tell a joke
in Latin, but anyone who has ever heard Latin jokes told in
high school knows that there are no funny ones. We smiled;
sometimes, when we really wanted something, we laughed.
But those chuckles were only a way of placating the wrath of
the termagant who was making us learn Latin whether we
wanted to or not. Certainly she did not feel limited to giving
us "positive reinforcement." On the second day of reading
Caesar's *Gallic Wars,* she asked one girl to translate a sentence.
The girl went through the sentence, describing the impedi-
menta with which the Helvetii moved and included, as I remember, horses, wagons, and baggage. There was a long
pause. Then Miss Filene started in on a severe lecture about the
use of "trots" or published translations. She pointed out that
Caesar had, indeed, listed the three items mentioned, but that
ours was an edited text that left out the baggage. She then
threatened us with all sorts of dire penalties if she caught any of
us using such trots. Then she went on to the next sentence.
The girl involved was reduced to lip-biting to hold back the
tears. She was the first that afternoon to list Miss Filene as the
best teacher we had had.

There is also another indication of the somewhat doubtful
relationship between teachers and student motivation. Almost every study done of college alumni five years or more
out of college indicates that graduates feel that freshman English was the most valuable course they had. I cannot believe
this is due to the fact that English teachers, including teaching
assistants and teaching fellows, are all that much better at
motivating students than other faculty members. The point
is that the subject matter of freshman composition is immediately applicable, and *that* is a built-in motivation for students.

Every teacher has the experience of getting lazy classes as well as hard-working classes. In the hard-working classes, the motivated classes, the teacher really has to do very little, except to provide the information. The students do the work. With lazy classes, there is almost nothing one can do. Over the years I have tried to do everything but stand on my head in class when I have been faced by an unmotivated class (and I suppose I would have tried to do that as well if I had ever learned how to do it). Ultimately I do not believe that there is anything one can do except wait out the semester. Older students are always more fun to teach than traditional-age students because they are motivated. They know why they are there, they know why they are taking the courses, and they are willing to work so that they can learn. It is for that reason that the greatest period of American college education was the four or five years following World War II, when the veterans returned to campuses.

There is an added argument against the idea that teachers can motivate students. Educationists talk about this subject more than anyone else. They talk about motivation not only to their students but to other faculty members. The only reason there are not more fist fights on campuses is that other faculty members are more tactful. I say this because education courses are, in my experience, universally disliked. They are universally uninteresting; they are universally looked upon as a waste of time. If the educationists think that you can motivate students and believe that they have a clue as to how to do it, why are their courses in such disrepute?

If it is possible for a faculty member to motivate a student, then the term probably implies some personal relationship beyond what is normally considered the teaching situation. Often that is simply a matter of luck or circumstance; sometimes, as I have said elsewhere, it is dangerous.

Often student motivation is simply a matter of timing in a student's life and probably, even more often than that, a matter of personal growth. The more we learn about stages of development in young people, the more we come to understand how motivation occurs within a large number of students. Perhaps just as much, it is a matter of choice. Any teacher who has to teach required courses as well as elective courses knows there is an immediate difference in the motivation of the students. In the elective courses, or in the courses given for majors, motivation is usually not a problem. The reason is that the students know why they are there, and they are motivated to do a good job. In the required courses the students do not know why they are there, in many cases, and do not want to be there. It is very difficult to "motivate" a student under those circumstances.

All that a teacher can do in any situation is his or her best and try to be interesting; for, although it is probably true that a teacher cannot provide motivation for a student, there is no doubt that a teacher can kill motivation in a student. The easiest way to do that is to subject the student to sheer boredom.

That Colleges Differ from One Another

I AM now so ancient that I can remember back when colleges were different from one another. It really made a difference where you went. It made a difference in teachers, it made a difference in students, it made a difference in curriculum, it made a difference in whether or not you learned your subject—whatever that might be. But it has been a long time since that was true. Now, I'm convinced, the only difference is the difference in the students you go to college with. I am not sure just when this change took place. I suspect it was during the late 50s, but it may not have occurred until the early 60s.

One of the things that happened in the late 50s and early 60s was that the number of students who went to college increased so rapidly that colleges that had never really thought about raising their standards—becoming "first rate"—found that they could do it. There were pretensions of grandeur alive in the land from coast to coast. Even the weakest colleges began to think that they were good. And that, of course, is part of what makes a really good college: it thinks it's good; its students think it's good. Whether it is or not depends not on the quality of the faculty, not even, I'm afraid, on the quality of the education in general, but whether the students think it is true or not. (I taught at one college for a number of years at which the students worked very hard because they believed the admissions standards were highly selective when, in fact, almost anyone who applied was accepted.) There is a long-time justification for that attitude. Anyone interested in it should read Cardinal Newman on

"The Idea of a University." It is the students that make the difference—and their attitude toward the college they are attending.

But my point is that sometime during this period, and especially in the 1960s, colleges began to look and feel like one another. For example, liberal arts colleges began to offer vocational courses. In 1948, when I started teaching at Middlebury College, there was one sure way of making certain that a course would be voted down by the faculty. All you had to do was to suggest that it had some practical benefits. The faculty would immediately mass together and vote it down: "That is vocational and has nothing to do with the liberal arts; therefore, let's get rid of it." Every college and university now has a vocational tinge to it (with the possible exception of St. John's College), and this is not the place to discuss whether that uniformity is good, bad, or indifferent. The point is that all colleges now look upon themselves as training grounds for the "real world."

The number of majors has altered, the quality of the majors has changed, and they do not differ very much from one college to another. We still have arguments about big colleges and small colleges, but one has to be very wary of those arguments. Robert Frost used to argue that he would rather learn sitting seventy-five feet away from a great mind than ten feet away from a third-rate one. That's a clever remark, and it may contain a great truth. But actually, "small" colleges today often do not provide the student with classes that are smaller than are the ones in the large universities. The result is that by choosing a small college, a student today may be opting to sit seventy-five feet away from a third-rate mind. On the other hand, at most larger universities today, students don't even have a chance to observe the great minds of the leading faculty for at least two years—two years spent in classes taught by teaching assistants who are worried about their own coursework and theses as much as they are about the students in their sections.

Two events brought home to me the basic similarity of all

institutions today. The first was the creation of an informal
network of correspondence in the late 60s which anchored in
David Riesman in Cambridge and included mutual friends
across the country. We found we could test what a college
year would be like simply by observing the climate on a
couple of different campuses. What immediately became apparent was that what was happening on one campus was
happening on all campuses. It made no difference whether
the college was male or female or coed, whether it was a
small liberal arts college or a multiversity. To use terms from
art appreciation, the tone and intensity of the political and
educational climates might be different, but the hues were the
same.

In the summer of 1970 all our previous discussions were
put to the test. The spring had been fearsome on most campuses. Violence had grown and reached a peak in the tragedy
of Kent State. Political activism had increased and many colleges decided that the way to head off further violence in the
fall would be to have an October break which allowed students to get home to work for candidates within the traditional election system. I had fought for just such a break at
Elmira College. I remember that David felt it was unnecessary, and, of course, he proved to be right.

When I crossed Harvard Yard in early August to get to the
social sciences building over by the Germanic Museum, I was
hit by two contrasting tonal "clues." (I remain a firm believer
in paying more attention to tone than to statistics in dealing
with any set of human relationships.) Out in the Square, as I
came out of the subway, I found a group of clean-shaven,
short-haired, well-dressed college age young people hawking
a mimeographed leaflet containing the names of all the shops
in the Boston area at which you could buy guns and other
kinds of weapons. That certainly boded ill for the following
months. Inside the yard, however, the SDS—that key core
group of student violence across the country—was holding a
cookie sale (I did not test the ingredients, but I was told they
were straight) to raise money for fall activities. That would

indicate to me that the college world had fallen back to normal with a near crash. In David's office, we talked about the conflicting signs all over the country and decided that there was no way to call it.

Two weeks later, Elmira opened, earlier than most colleges because of a freshman program that began well before the upperclassmen returned. Within a week it was clear that nothing was going to happen at Elmira that year, and I wrote to David and others and said that the academic year across the country would be absolutely peaceful. These students would do nothing, even if Nixon declared war on Mars. It was David's turn to be skeptical. But that is exactly what happened.*

It really has been possible ever since the 60s to test what is happening on all campuses by looking carefully at any one campus. And that generalization holds for attitudes toward classes, student morale, participation in student activities, and all the rest.

The other event, even more eye-opening, although it contained nothing essentially new, was an evening spent sitting around in a Rome hotel room with some thirty admissions directors from all different kinds of colleges and universities. We were on a tour of European private international schools and American overseas military schools, looking for candidates for the following year. Everyone else was looking at twelfth graders. I was looking at tenth graders, as I was then president of Simon's Rock, a four-year college beginning after the tenth grade.

After a certain number of beers, glasses of wine, and stronger drinks, someone suggested that we ought to put together *the* American-institution-of-higher-education catalog. Everyone jumped in with glee. In the next few hours we

---

*It should be made clear that Professor Riesman does not share my view of the basic similarity of colleges across the country. Even at the time he felt there were more than simply shades of difference among them, although he had said that most of them were more successful in imitating each other than in being different.

had not only established the order and contents of the catalog, but also inserted all the pictures (a long shot down library stacks to a boy/girl sitting silhouetted against a window; a teacher sitting on his desk talking earnestly, obviously
about literature; a teacher pointing earnestly at a blackboard
filled with mathematical formulas; two students walking
down a shady path with arms/hands entwined, and so on). It
was easy. But then the real fun started. We wrote the president's opening remarks to the students, set up the calendar,
put in the fee schedules (leaving blanks for institutional differences that would actually be several thousand dollars),
wrote up the academic requirements with all the loopholes,
described the college's position on *in loco parentis,* described
the student government, residential groups, scholarships,
and so on. Not content with this, we drew up the list of
majors and minors, listed the requirements, and then began
to write the course descriptions. It was true. You really can
write the all-American college catalog (again, excluding St.
John's).

There are several reasons for this change; among them, and
perhaps the most important, is the fact that almost any college (or for that matter, junior college) can now hire an entire
faculty of Ph.D.s, men and women with common backgrounds in graduate work in America. It is not surprising,
therefore, that their attitudes toward college teaching and
college offerings should be similar. Another factor is that on
most college campuses, although many administrations
would not admit it, something like a publish-or-perish attitude has become accepted. This means that a large number of
faculty members will be spending a considerable portion of
their time doing their own research rather than spending the
vast amounts of time with their students that they used to.

There is another reason, and one of the most dangerous
reasons, for the similarity today. With the decrease in the
pool of potential students coming out of high schools, colleges have begun to fight with each other at a level that
sometimes reminds one more of the selling of soap than of

the recruiting of students. As a result, when a college discovers a gimmick, a ploy, or even an occasional genuinely new educational program that will draw students to a college, the admissions personnel immediately notify the administration and faculty on other college campuses, and it is not long before all the other colleges, at least in the same region, have similar programs, ploys, or gimmicks. This process leads to a watering down of curricula and a general lowering of standards. And that lowering of standards is simply made worse by the decreasing student pool, which is decreasing ever more sharply. All colleges are being affected by this decrease, although certainly not to the same extent. Harvard, Yale, Brown, and other highly selective colleges are still getting first-rate students, but as the pool from which they draw grows smaller, they are also drawing students away from the second level of college choices. The second level colleges are therefore having to draw from the third level, and so on down the line.

One of the most frightening elements in all this is that although all colleges know it is happening, the grades given by faculty are remaining as high as they were during the period of grade inflation during the late 60s and early 70s. In other words, grades simply do not mean the same now as they did twenty years ago.

There are two very practical results to recognizing the similarity among colleges, and they are results that ought to be recognized by high school students and their parents. They should, of course, be recognized even more by high school guidance counselors, but that unfortunately is not the case in general. The first is that the importance of a given choice of college is not what it is reputed to be. Among New England private schools there is a pathetic, nay sometimes tragic, day called Black Monday, the day on which the acceptance announcements arrive from all the leading colleges and universities. It is disheartening to see absolutely first-rate students standing around with tears in their eyes because they have been turned down by, say, Harvard, and *only* accepted by Yale and Princeton. This kind of nonsense only insures that the edge of excitement that should accompany the beginning of college by any student is sometimes ruined by false snobbery. Unfortunately, parents often make the situation worse rather than better when they lead their children to believe that some form of disaster has occurred when the college that the *parent* thinks is the *right* school is not the college that accepts the child, even though it is likely that the child will do better at the school by which he or she has been accepted.

The second result is that one really should not worry so much about which college any student goes to. If, as I have suggested, most colleges today are really very much alike, then it means that a student will be able to get just about the same education no matter where he or she goes. I think that is literally true. It has probably always been true that a student gets out of college exactly what he puts into it. It is certainly true today, and it is true throughout the whole range of American colleges and universities. There are very few small colleges without some faculty members that make an absolutely superb education possible; and unless one searches out good teaching faculty on major university campuses, it is possible to receive an absolutely dreadful education there.

Luckily, there is, in American education, a way of saving a poor decision. A student can always transfer after the first two years. As a matter of fact, it makes very good sense to go to a small college and get more personal attention from really good teachers in introductory courses, and then to transfer to a larger university for the leading scholars that one meets in upper division classes.

I

That College Professors Are Liberal

ONE of the ideas that most college teachers have about themselves and their profession, and one that is certainly shared by the community in general, is that college professors are liberals. That is patently false. I am not, of course, talking about what ticket they vote in November every four years. I'm talking about the way they think in general. One of the qualities of liberalism is that it thinks freely and is willing to alter when new information comes in; it is open to new ideas and experimentation. Certainly that is not the governing characteristic of many college professors. Sometimes, of course, it does have political implications. When I came back from Europe in 1953 and started teaching at the University of Vermont, I sat through a series of faculty meetings that were absolutely appalling to me. It was the middle of the McCarthy era, and faculty members everywhere were running scared. At one point I watched that otherwise fine faculty—it was one of the best I have ever taught with—vote themselves into a position in which Pablo Picasso would not be allowed to teach art or painting. That is the kind of idiocy up with which I find it hard to put.

But more often faculty members' conservatism shows up in an unwillingness to alter the status quo of the educational program. A typical situation developed at Colby College the next year. Colby was granted one of those Ford Foundation grants to undergo a self-study, and immediately many of the best faculty were placed on a committee to review the whole curriculum. They came up with a long, detailed, and remarkably thoughtful series of recommendations. During the next three months of faculty meetings, I watched the faculty systematically defeat every one of the recommendations of the Self-Study Committee. The usual winning argument was by an older member of the faculty, a really delightful person and excellent Hardy scholar, who almost always began, "In the thirty-five years that I have taught here . . ." And down would go another proposal.

On most college campuses there is considerable lip service paid to interdisciplinary work of one sort or another. Actually, interdisciplinary work succeeds only on those campuses on which administrations give the interdisciplinary programs so much support that faculty members do not feel they can vote it down. Usually it means that an individual faculty member who wants to teach in an interdisciplinary way, and has the credentials to convince a large number of the faculty that he is able to, takes over. But the moment that he leaves, the program disappears.

I have in my more cynical moments decided that there is a generalization that works in American college education—or education at any level in America, for that matter—which goes: Any successful experiment will be voted out as soon as possible. I can think of three examples immediately. The Harvard General Education Program was established by a small committee with the backing of the president. A number of the faculty immediately set their minds to getting rid of it. When a vote came on the introductory biology course, which was one of the key elements of the program, the vote went against the course, and a voice was heard from the back of the room, "One down, two to go."

At San Jose State, as I have mentioned elsewhere, an experiment took place which was the most carefully set up and most successfully documented experiments in the teaching of writing that I know of in American educational history. After three years with quite remarkable results, the faculty voted the experiment out. At Elmira College, the Liberal Studies Program not only raised enrollment, but clearly raised the level of participation of students in their own educations. There was a kind of educational excitement that was quite catching. It too was voted out by the faculty at the earliest possible moment.

There is a reason for this behavior, but it is an unfortunate one. Experimental programs of any kind take extra work on the part of the faculty. For one thing, it means they have to revamp their entire approach to the subject matter, whatever it might be. And second, it threatens the Establishment on any campus. These are not good reasons to be against any educational program, but they are real ones.

The question, then, is whether there is a difference between the educational conservatism of faculty members and their political positions. Not really. There is an old Republican adage that if you want to change somebody into a conservative, you give him money to manage. That has a remarkable amount of truth to it. The change in the political position of American faculty members occurred during the 60s. There are some who will argue they were driven into conservatism by fear of the various student movements, and that may, indeed, have had something to do with it. But perhaps more important, they were suddenly making more money than they had in the past. Teachers' salaries, at least at the college level, began to approach those of other jobs, although certainly not other professions. It is certainly remarkable how conservative the ownership of stock makes many faculty members. I began to see that in the early 60s at Case Institute, but even more so in the late 60s in Wyoming and in New York.

I wouldn't want to be misunderstood. I think there is something about the educational process that does keep teachers young and liberal. But it is wrong to think that people come into teaching with a pre-set liberal position. One of my favorite quotations to describe the educational situation on many college campuses is not one that I made up myself, although I would have loved to. I owe it to John Satterfield, who came as provost at Elmira College after being on the faculty of Florida Presbyterian, now Eckard Col-

lege. John described the usual situation quickly and suc-
cinctly. He said most college faculties are made up of the Old
Turks and the Young Guard.

When I was doing a Ford Foundation study of humanities
programs in engineering institutions, it struck me over and
over again that the teachers who held the most liberal positions, who were most open to the consideration of new ideas,
were those who had been around a long time. The real tradi-
tionalists were young men and women just out of graduate
school. They were waving the banners of their disciplines
and felt they would not be able to hold up their heads among
their peers at the annual national meetings if they were not
teaching the same courses in the same way as their colleagues
at every other institution. For all their liberal political protes-
tations, they were the preservers of their own immediate
past.

J

That Frontiersmen Were Brave

HAVING grown up with a father who wished that he had been born and raised on a ranch in the West and having spent most of my Saturday afternoons as a child at the movies, wallowing in the deeds of Hollywood cowboys as they won the West, I grew up with the idea that cowboys and western men in general were strong, silent types who fought for what they believed in openly and bravely, often on the main street of town at high noon. Gary Cooper in *The Virginian* was only a model of what all such men did naturally: fight it out with their enemies in single combat in plain view of all. I was wrong.

In the fall of 1964 I left San Francisco State College, where I had been Dean of Humanities, Language, and Literature, and headed for the English department of the University of Wyoming. When I talked with Walter Van Tilburg Clark, the wonderful author of *Track of the Cat* and *The Ox-bow Incident* who was head of the Creative Writing Program at San Francisco, and told him that it looked as though I were heading back east again, he said, "Baird, no matter what the map says, when you move from San Francisco to Laramie, Wyoming, you're headed west."

I was one of some fifty faculty members and administrators who went to the University of Wyoming that year. The retiring president, who had been there many years, realized that he had built up the university physically, but he really hadn't brought it up to date academically. The way he put it to me and others was: "I want you to bring the university into the twentieth century." Two years later almost all of us had left. We figured that we had brought the place up to about 1805, and the residents of the state—and a number of the older faculty—couldn't stand it. (That may be an unjust criticism.)

But my point is a bit different. Soon after I got there, a group of students began to tell me about the injustices that often occurred on the campus of the university of "The Equality State." For example, we found out that if a white girl were seen talking with one of the black athletes on campus, one of the housemothers took it upon herself to write or call the parents of the girl and tell them that their daughter had been seen socializing with a black person. There were also a number of inequities around town. It was almost impossible for a minority student to find an apartment to rent. One of the most surprising discoveries to me was to find that an absolutely beautiful girl on campus, who turned out to be Miss Indian America for that year or the year before, felt that the only students she could talk with were minority students from other parts of the country. They were the only ones who could understand the situation she found herself in. Of course, I couldn't even tell that she was an Indian, whatever that meant.

At any rate, we started a local civil liberties group. It was the mid-60s, and the political temperature was still lukewarm—especially in Wyoming—but there was a strong sense of political justice hanging over from the Kennedy days, and the antiwar feelings about Vietnam were beginning to grow, and grow quickly. Teach-ins had begun to spring up around the country, and Wyoming was one of the first universities to hold a large-scale teach-in, although we were careful to have representatives from both sides take part in the programs. One of the reasons for that evenhandedness was that Senator Gale McGee, who had formerly been on the faculty of the university, was one of those who tested positions for Lyndon Johnson when he was preparing to escalate American participation in Southeast Asia.

The president of the university, who had just arrived from

Vermont, and was to go back very quickly when he discovered that the conservatism of Vermont, which was basically economic, and the conservatism of Wyoming, which
was political, had little to do with one another, was in no
way averse to the activities of the civil liberties group. He
merely asked that when we discovered violations of anyone's
rights, we would first work through the regular processes of
the university before we went public with our complaints.
Naturally, we agreed. I might add that most of the students
involved in the group were from the East, from New York
and New Jersey, although some of the strongest members
were from Wyoming. Every one of the problems that we
uncovered, we were able to clear up—and clear up quickly—
through normal university channels. We never even had to
go to the university's paper, much less the local Laramie
newspaper. That is the good side of the story.

The bad side is that as we began to act on complaints, and
only the most obvious complaints, such as that of a leading
black student (a fine young man with excellent grades) who
was not able to find an apartment, although there were many
available in the town at the time (and the previously mentioned case of the housemother); word spread among the
college students about what we were doing and there were,
threats of violence. I personally had no problems as a result of
my involvement with this group, but almost all the students
who worked with us were threatened at one time or another.
The threats were not of immediate physical violence but instead almost always took the form of "Wait till I get you this
summer when I've got a gun strapped on my belt." The
threats were of physical violence some time in the future for
which a student could not prepare without breaking the law.
Students who were threatened were, naturally, frightened. I
should add that being frightened did not keep them from
continuing to fight for the civil rights of others although they
felt—and I had to agree with them—that the threats were
meant very seriously. If one were around the streets of a
Wyoming town during the summer or during a vacation

period, it was not unusual to see a student who had been dressed like other undergraduates while on campus walking around with a six-gun strapped to his side.

Physical violence, death by shooting, was not unusual in those days. In the city of Laramie shootings took place quite regularly, but as most of them took place within minority communities, the police were not terribly concerned. As one police officer admitted to me at a party one night, "As long as they kill themselves, we don't really care."

I think it is fair to say that in the Old West, one man did indeed come up to another and say, "I'll meet you at high noon on the main street, and we'll settle our differences by shooting it out." But after my experiences in the West, I'm convinced that at about 11:55, one or both of those men were hiding behind rain barrels at the side of the street, waiting for the other to put in an appearance, unguarded, in the middle of the dusty thoroughfare.

As a postscript or footnote to this account, I should like to add the story of the head of the ROTC Detachment at Wyoming while I was there: a first-rate pilot, a marvelous man, a man with a real feeling for the needs of others. He and I were bitterly opposed as far as United States involvement in Vietnam was concerned. Whenever there was a teach-in or any public debate about the war, we would oppose each other with great vigor. Members of the community seemed surprised when, on Sunday afternoons, he and I would be out together raising money for the Episcopal church. He sported a presidential citation as a member of the Strategic Air Command (SAC) group that carried atomic bombs on the raid against China—luckily aborted—that Eisenhower sent to bring the final conflict in Korea to an end.

There were a great many citizens of Laramie who did not approve of my stand on the conflict in Vietnam, which is not surprising, but that does not mean that they rejected me as a person. Even Gale McGee, about whom I said very few nice things during the early days of the conflict in Vietnam (although we were personal friends), was willing to give a speech in the United States Senate about the nature of free speech and inquiry on a university campus referring to my problems in Laramie. But my ROTC colonel friend made the really big mistake in "The Equality State." He helped sponsor a Job Corps Ranch to help bring poor black kids from Chicago out to the West to learn how to do ranching and farming on a ranch not far from Laramie. A number of the good citizens of Laramie and the surrounding area put pressure on the Air Force to get him out of the state. He never did find out who was making the complaints about him. No one faced him personally to complain about his helping out with the Job Corps program, although he heard through other people that there was unhappiness with his activities. But they effectively got rid of him, although it may not have been with a six-gun on the hip during the summer. But his removal, like that other threat, was certainly not just a symbolic gesture. And it certainly was no face-to-face conflict on the main street in open confrontation.

K

That the Northeast Is More Liberal

WHEN Spiro Agnew—does anyone remember the name?—was Vice-President of the United States, and cute alliterative phrases blossomed forth from the White House, he often referred to the "Eastern Liberal Effete." What he was referring to, of course, was faculty members and graduates of northeastern colleges. But it was not only Agnew who foisted this kind of generalization on the American people. It is still being said in one way or another by many politicians, sociologists, and so on. Even the college faculty of most northeastern universities pride themselves on being liberal, or at least more liberal than faculties in the rest of the country. Some of them consider the rest of the country backwards or even "slow." But in educational terms, this myth of liberalness is simply not the case, or at best is misleading.

Educational experiment of almost any worthwhile kind requires liberal attitudes. It requires a willingness on the part of faculty members to let go of established practices, to let go of established departmental and disciplinary attitudes. Having taught at colleges everywhere from Maine to Hawaii, I have found that such liberal attitudes toward educational experimentation grow as you cross the Hudson River and head west. It is present only in its most superficial forms in New England.

An open attitude toward experimentation and liberal approaches to education seems to me to show up most clearly in relation to interdisciplinary courses and interdisciplinary majors, such as American Studies. In the Northeast, such majors as American Studies are most often a collection of traditional disciplinary courses stuck together in some larger grouping, and even the grouping turns out to be a rather thinly disguised History or English major, with a minor in the other subject. As one moves to the Midwest, and even more to the Far West, the American Studies major tends to become much more genuinely interdisciplinary, and faculty members are much more likely to bring together the various disciplines in a course. Moreover, the farther west one goes, the more one runs into the willingness to include the creative arts in such a major. Even the Southwest, a section of the country most often considered conservative or reactionary by people in the Northeast, is much more open to experiment than most New England colleges are.

In the East, a teacher who wishes to try to experiment finds himself immediately running up against disciplinary and departmental barriers. A friend of mine who has taught at a New England liberal arts college for nearly forty years was recently congratulating himself and being extremely pleased that at last he had been able to convince his departmental colleagues and the college that he should be free to use literary works as the basic readings for a history course. Big deal! That, of course, has been a common practice in humanities courses and interdisciplinary courses as well as many history courses throughout the United States for at least fifty years. Indeed, at San Francisco State, as an opposite example, membership in many departments was encouraged by the administration and by members of the faculty as well. The situation is by no means new. Professor Houston Peterson was constantly under attack by the English Department at Rutgers in the 30s and 40s because he approached major philosophical issues by using great novels as his texts.

If a student is looking for a genuine humanities major, he should not look to the Northeast; he should look toward a place like San Francisco State, where the humanities major has been around for some thirty years. Or he should look at Evergreen State College, in Olympia, Washington, where all of the programs are genuinely interdisciplinary and team-taught. These programs are not just collections of disciplinary courses grouped in such a way that they look interdisciplinary. They are programs of core courses and advanced seminars in which genuine interdisciplinary study is pursued at some depth, at the same time that the student major is able to pursue a specific discipline as well, often in the form of independent study.

None of this is meant as a condemnation of the traditional methods of education, nor of disciplines, nor of standard departments. But it seems to me that if anyone is going to be self-satisfied about something, he ought to be satisfied about the right thing. Being satisfied about the wrong thing is intellectually dishonest. At least in terms of experimental education, the Northeast can not make any claims about being more liberal, or even as liberal, as the rest of the country.

L

That the New Right Is Fundamentalist

I GREW up among a group of genuine fundamentalists. They were the real thing. They believed in the verbal inspiration of the Bible. They believed in the literalness of God's Word. And they tried, and tried their best, to live up to their beliefs. I see no visible connection between those people and the New Right.

Perhaps a case in point would be helpful. I learned New Testament Greek from a man named Mr. Bishop, who worked at the New Brunswick Seminary of the Reformed Church. Mr. Bishop had been a Reformed minister in North Jersey during the 1920s and had been fired from his pulpit. Mr. Bishop was one of those late Victorian gentlemen who always wore a starched wing-collar and morning coat. He once told me that he did not keep a telephone in his apartment because he didn't know what he would do if the telephone rang while he was praying. He did not think it was funny when I laughed. But during his term as minister to a congregation that was far more theologically liberal than he was, one of the members told him she was presenting a paper to the local WCTU on the fact that the Bible was against drinking. She wanted Mr. Bishop to let his name be used as a sponsor for her paper. Mr. Bishop said that he might, but he wanted to read the paper first. Being the honest man that he was, he went back carefully through the Bible. Not surprisingly, he discovered that the overwhelming number of references to drinking in the Bible are in favor of it. Very few are against it, and these are against its misuse rather than its use. When he told the woman he could not sponsor her paper, she was understandably offended. But Mr. Bishop was not the type to leave the situation there. The next Sunday he gave a sermon about the Bible's position on drinking. As a great many in his congregation were members of the WCTU, and as the sale of alcoholic beverages was at that time still illegal, the congregation felt that he was not a proper minister for their church. I once asked him if he himself ever drank, and he answered that he had a small glass of sherry every four or five years just to show that he wasn't prejudiced.

The old style fundamentalist followed the Bible remarkably well. He knew that he should not be conformed to society, and he knew St. Paul meant just that when he wrote it. That is no longer true. The New Right spends most of its time conforming. I think the shift came with television. Before television, fundamentalists took a pretty strong position on such things as dancing and the movies. Again following St. Paul, they wanted to avoid any behavior that might possibly lead a weak brother to offend. Whether they were right or not is a different point. I suspect that David would not have shared their feelings about dancing, although Michal might have. They recognized that movies often contained a potential threat to their own behavior and thoughts. And the movie theater posters of scantily clad heroines like Theda Bara, Clara Bow, and Jean Harlow convinced them that something was happening in those theaters which they could not condone.

When the television set entered the home, a whole new world opened to them. Even if they attempted to avoid movies they had previously refused to see in the theaters, the other programs, especially the soap operas, provided them with examples of all the human behavior they needed. And then, instead of reacting against the medium, they decided to use it. And they decided to use it in all the ways that the medium used them. I can remember that Jezebel was often referred to as an example of the evils of the overuse of makeup. I personally preferred Hamlet's rejoinder to Ophelia, "God hath given you one face, and you make yourselves another." But the point is that the overuse of makeup as a sign of substituting the world's standards for God's was pretty much a constant among fundamentalists. Nowadays, television stars on so-called Christian networks come on with enough makeup, especially eye makeup, to remind one of the old British description, "her eyes looked like two holes burned in a blanket."

Fundamentalists used to believe that one should not take too much heed of the morrow. Sometimes they went remarkably far. I remember one minister who preached a sermon against buying insurance because it indicated a lack of trust in God. But now both Christian television and radio networks offer programs in investment counseling which are sometimes more strident in their tone than anything that "pagan" investment counselors suggest. There is not only no trust in God; there is a plentiful lack of belief in Christian practices in business indicated in those programs.

Fundamentalists believed in education up to the last decade or so, and they did not try to ruin it. They went to the seventeenth chapter of John and learned that Christ prayed that his followers should be kept in the world and not taken out of it; so they believed that they should fight for their own beliefs in this world rather than change the world, except through preaching and acting according to their own beliefs. As a matter of fact they often exercised a very healthy influence on teaching. They knew that wisdom and knowledge were related. It is for that reason that small German communities often had such remarkably good educational programs—and still do.

But today the New Right seems to spend most of its time trying to wreck local education programs. They set themselves up as censors of material that all students should read. I know of one Texas town—and there are probably hundreds—in which the teachers are utterly afraid in their daily classroom activities. The reason is that the administration and the school board do not listen to them or to what they feel should be done with the educational program. Instead they listen to the minister and congregation of the First Baptist Church. And when one of the members of the New Right enters the classroom as teacher, some appalling things often occur. I can think of one teacher who uses *Death of a Salesman* in class but inks out the climax scene in the Boston hotel room. I have never discovered how the students are supposed to understand the play. In another case the teacher will not allow the word "liquor" to be used in class. The students must use the word "medicine" instead.

But above all, the fundamentalists I grew up with were for peace, not for war. They believed in the Sermon on the Mount. They paid attention to the fact that one of the beatitudes was "Blessed are the peacemakers." And if they did not always follow it, any more than others do, they at least tried. They did not preach hatred. They did not preach armaments. They did not preach the killing of the poor, the downtrodden, the helpless, of Central American or southeast Asian countries. Or the potential destruction of the world through nuclear warfare. And they certainly did not preach the use of retaliatory weapons for the destruction of mankind. They paid attention to Christ's command not to return evil for evil.

That Hopelessness Breeds Revolution

I DO not intend to introduce any startlingly new material in this discussion. But I am concerned, as I am so often, that we have forgotten the lessons of the 1960s, both in societal and in educational terms. During the recent recession, for example, news broadcasters talked about the large number of unemployed as a potential source of revolutionary behavior, especially those unemployed who had fallen off the back side of unemployment benefits and, in a sense, disappeared from public consciousness. Comparisons have been made with the lot of the Polish worker or member of Solidarity. But during the 1960s we discovered a very important fact about human behavior: raised expectations, not hopelessness, bring about revolutionary behavior. There was nothing really new here. The traditional view of despair in all allegories was that it rendered the person who fell into its clutches absolutely helpless. As a matter of fact, despair was, in the Middle Ages, often referred to as the unforgivable sin, as its subject felt that not even God could raise a man's hopes.

In actual fact, most long-term recessions breed calm if not despair. As more and more people go off the public support rolls in the opposite direction, into anonymity and despond, that group of people is apparently not a cause of worry for society. I do not mean by that that they are not to be pitied or to be cared for, but they are not likely to be the source of any revolutionary activity, especially if the recession is widespread.

On the other hand, society is faced by the uncomfortable fact that genuine progress brings with it an impetus toward revolution because it raises hope and expectations among the poor and downtrodden. Such an impetus frightens people, especially people who are comfortable in the present situation, whatever it is; but the fear is a fear based on a movement toward a better future.

In education, hopelessness leads to the acceptance of things as they are, no matter how bad they may be. It also leads to a deadening of the inquiring spirit. When administrations, or boards of trustees, or school boards show that they will not listen, teachers often simply stop trying. Perhaps even more important these days, they simply leave the teaching profession. The problem is compounded by the fact that very often the ones who leave the profession are the best teachers. But the administrator who does not listen or who follows his own unbending course of action is not the only cause of hopelessness among teachers. Just as debilitating is what I refer to as the pillow administrator, one to whom any complaint is like punching a pillow. There is no reaction at all. A "yes" can mean anything; a "maybe" does mean anything. After a while, a faculty member simply gives up.

Progress in education is always uncomfortable, and it ought to be. When an administration is having an easy time of it, its members ought to be ashamed of themselves. It means that nothing is happening. Right now schools across the country are losing many of their very best teachers. Low teacher salaries are certainly one cause, but only one cause, and I am not even sure that it is the most important cause. As I talk to young teachers (and some not so young) who are leaving the profession, I find that it is when administrators stop listening or when they turn aside genuine discussions of educational ideas that the good teachers begin to think about doing something else. There is often another result, of course, that is even more tragic to everyone concerned, especially the students: teachers sometimes simply die on the job. They give up and go through their work mechanically and repetitively.

Criticism of education by presidential commissions, or

state commissions, or board commissions, in itself will do absolutely nothing. Certainly the repetition in speeches of old maxims or saws—once described by Ambrose Bierce as being so-named because they made their way through a wooden head—by a president or a political candidate will not bring about any real changes. Only when there is a sign of genuine hope, when there is a feeling of raised expectations, will positive changes come about that will help American education at all levels out of its present doldrums. What many false-economy-minded politicians fail to realize is that funding at any level is a positive sign to teachers, parents, and students alike that governments mean what they say. It becomes a visible measure of raised expectations. I know of several college presidents who are always surprised when they do not get faculty support when they announce a new idea or program and then add, "But, of course, we can not give this any more funding." Certainly it has always been true of American political and social—and educational—policy that where our treasure has been placed, there our hearts have been also.

That Being Relevant Is Relevant

DURING the 1970 Hamilton College conference for new teachers there was a valuable study session with some ten or fifteen Hamilton College students. The question that most of the young teachers wanted to ask was the one that was most current at the moment: what did students mean when they demanded that the courses they took should be relevant? It was fascinating to listen to the answers, as there was no agreement among the students as to what they meant. One thing that *was* immediately apparent was that they did not mean they wanted anything vocational. They were not asking to be trained for specific jobs. Another clear agreement in their answers was that they had no practical solutions to offer to the new college teachers.

Three hours of general talk led to the conclusion on the part of those involved, including the students, that what students really seemed to mean by "being relevant" was being interesting, or, in their terms, providing motivation. One can hardly argue with such a desire. It is important, however, to repeat that they were in no way arguing for vocationalism. I will deal with that issue in another essay.

If the goal of education is learning to think, then any subject is, or can be, "relevant." It depends on how it is taught. It also depends on the attitude of the students in a course, however. Perhaps most interesting among the comments of the students was the revelation that the timeframe of the course material was really not important. I think that most of us in college teaching at the time felt that the students meant that nothing was relevant unless it had occurred during the past three-and-one-half minutes. The more the discussion went on, however, the more it became apparent that the timeframe was not crucial. And it certainly should not be. If we are talking about what is relevant or what is helpful in the process of learning to think, then there is certainly no restriction on the time period of the subject. It has often been said that all of philosophy is a series of footnotes to Plato and Aristotle. That still remains a cogent observation for me. We have talked so much in our culture about progress that we sometimes forget that progress is a sometime thing.

In working on a book of great beginnings in literature, I was suddenly struck by the fact that the first two poems that we have in Western Civilization are the *Iliad* and the *Odyssey*. There are no poems that are greater than these two. A colleague of mine read a passage I was writing and said, "Oh come now, are you saying that the *Iliad* and the *Odyssey* are the greatest poems ever written?" I pointed out that that was not what I had said, but if he wanted to push me on the issue, I'd probably have to say they were. The point remains that there are no *greater* poems than the *Iliad* and the *Odyssey,* and they are the first ones we have. Artists continue to go back to Magdalenian cave paintings for inspiration. The deer and bison are treated with such care and delicacy, the use of line and color is so precise and sophisticated, that one really cannot argue that the art of painting has ever reached a higher level. Men still lead their lives, in every major religion, according to the dictates, the lives, the beliefs of religious leaders of two thousand years ago, and longer.

And yet it is true that during the 1960s, history had a bad name. I have never quite understood why that was true. At Case Institute in the 1950s, I never had any trouble convincing groups of engineers that Thucydides' *History of the Peloponnesian Wars* was one of the most important books of history ever written, and that they could still learn from the lessons of that book. In the 1960s I could hardly get students to read the thing, much less feel that it was relevant.

There is always the danger that a teacher will give in to the search for relevancy in the teaching of his subject without finding out what the students really mean. College professors sometimes still act as if the matter of relevancy were important in the manner in which they understood the term in the 1960s, and the results are often damaging. For example, freshman composition textbooks of rhetoric and readings have increasingly contained a very high proportion of sheer junk in an attempt to be "relevant." One of the encouraging changes of the past two or three years has been the return of really good selections to the freshman composition texts. Of course, relevancy is not always the deciding issue in this matter of choosing writing examples. I had a high school English teacher who believed that you should read examples of poor writing along with pieces of good writing. I did not agree with her then, and I still think she was wrong. All of us come in contact with enough examples of poor writing day after day to need as many examples of good writing as we can get, especially in a freshman composition course. The choice of readings for college textbooks, or for high school textbooks, should be the best of any age and should not be limited simply to the present. Swift's *A Modest Proposal* can still turn a group of high school or college students as green as any book like *Lord of the Flies,* or even recent bloodletting movies like the *Friday the 13th* series.

I am certainly not arguing in any of these comments that there should be no contemporary pieces in textbooks. But the choice should not be made on the basis of whether a selection is modern or old. For example, if I am making selections for a freshman English course, I still find E. B. White and James Thurber among the best prose stylists the English language has produced. The fact that they are funnier than other writers is quite beside the point.

As in so many cases, there is a real lesson to be learned from the question of relevance. I learned it teaching engineers at Case. Teaching humanities to a group of engineers was a remarkable experience. The first few days were given over, whether explicitly or implicitly, to the problem of why they were sitting in that course at all. Why were they not in mathematics and science courses rather than in humanities classes? Most of the students were quite willing to express their unhappiness openly. I found, and still find, the situation quite healthy. Teachers, like preachers, have an obligation, it seems to me, to those whom they teach to show why what they are studying is important for their lives, why it will affect them and change them, why it will make life more worthwhile. Why should it not be our obligation as teachers to show the relevancy of our material to our students? After all, it is only when we find books relevant or interesting that we continue to read them ourselves.

That Research and Publication
Are Not Necessary for Good Teaching

BACK in the summer of 1950, a friend of mine who was
in the history department of Middlebury and I were talking with his father-in-law, the great Zechariah Chafee, Jr., of
the Harvard Law School and author of some of the best
statements on freedom of the press in this century. As usual,
we were complaining about the doctrine of publish-or-perish
in American college education. We were both young, idealis-
tic, and unpublished. Professor Chafee put it this way: If
anyone is going to be a good teacher, he is going to have
ideas that he wants other people to know and think about.
Just stating those ideas to students is not good enough. They
have to be tested against other minds who know as much
about a subject as the teacher does. Since then, I have often
thought about Professor Chafee's statement, and I have to
agree that it is true. A person who does not have ideas that he
wants his peers to think about is probably not a very good
teacher.

The danger of the publish-or-perish concept, then, is not
the concept itself but the timing that is involved. If a college
requires someone to publish according to a timetable, the
result is likely to be what it turns out to be most of the time—
dreadful. One should publish when he is ready to publish and
not before. I recognize that there is a practical problem here,
as far as college administrations are concerned. But if they
know their faculty as well as they should before they grant
tenure, they should be able to make some reasonably sound

judgments about whether someone is going to publish anything in the future or not.

Mr. Chafee's son-in-law is a good case in point. Pardon Tillinghast did not publish for many years although he was constantly doing research. I know of no teacher in my experience who spent his summers more beneficially than Pardon. He read constantly, kept voluminous notes, and in general made me feel lazy in comparison. It was genuine research; but it was not publishable in the accepted sense. It was research for the classroom.

But that, of course, is one element of research as far as teaching is concerned. The major purpose of research for a teacher should be in keeping abreast of the field, keeping up with all of the latest information, finding out what has been proved wrong, discovering what new ideas have come to the fore. In other words, it means keeping alive. One can not put a timetable on keeping alive.

But it is important that a teacher continue to do research in whatever form that may take. One reason is that students need models, and simply being a teacher is a model only for other teachers or future teachers. What students need is a model for research, not just the rules for research. Simply presenting the rules is always a very real danger. Anyone who thinks that he is communicating research methods simply by teaching research methods is missing an important point. Research methods in themselves can be weary, stale, and unprofitable. They can even be dangerous. They can put the emphasis in the wrong place. They can end up, as they have in one school system that I know, by teaching students to footnote every sentence in a so-called research paper.

I have already recounted the famous story about William James when an elderly woman came up to him after an evening lecture in Cambridge and asked him what he thought about a given subject. James paused very briefly and then answered, "I don't know. I haven't said anything yet." This is the case with most of us. There are very few of us who can genuinely meditate, who can sit and think through a subject on our own. Most of us fall into reverie of one form or another. The only times that we really do much clear thinking is when we are speaking to others or writing. One of the problems with teaching is that the teacher is always thinking—or should be—of the response of the students. Therefore, the teacher's thoughts are not necessarily as clear or concise as they should be. It is when the teacher is himself writing that he finds out what he really thinks. Students, while they are good listeners, are not a sufficient check on the ideas of teachers.

I left America and American graduate work in 1951 because I refused to get the "union card" that I felt the American Ph.D. stood for. I still think that that is the situation to a great extent. At the University of Edinburgh I found that once you were accepted for thesis work, you were treated as an intellectual peer by the faculty and were judged by the same rigorous standard. I have come to believe that the thesis for the Ph.D. is a good requirement for college teaching, although that requirement should always be modified by the insertion of the qualifying phrase "or its equivalent" in order to take into consideration both the creative artists and those who have gone on to research and publication without benefit of graduate coursework. The great Shakespearean scholar Lyman Kittredge, M.A., remains a lesson for all who would substitute hard and fast rules for enlightened requirements with his famous retort to the question of why he did not get a Ph.D.: "Who would examine me?"

The reason that the Ph.D. is a good requirement for college teaching is that it means that a person has submitted to the judgment of his peers. While I was English Department Chairman at San Francisco State, I would occasionally have some well-intentioned person come into the office clutching a notebook of typed poetry or prose to his or her bosom. When asked if they had published anything, the response was often, "Nothing, but I'd be happy to have you read my work." That's not enough. If a person wants to be hired to teach creative writing, that person ought to be willing and able to put his work out to be judged by his peers.

The trouble with the doctrine of publish-or-perish as it is practiced in American colleges and universities is that it is seen, as is much of the work for the Ph.D., as a series of roadblocks through which one has to pass to receive tenure or promotion. There are too few journals for the number of faculty members who are seeking to remain on university faculties. And most of those journals have rather rigid rules as to what they will accept, leaving the teacher who wants to try a new approach out in left field somewhere. There should be, as there now is in many regions of the United States, a system which allows for good papers, well presented, to take the place of the usual publications. In Texas, for example, there are many regional organizations which allow faculty— probably as many as are ready to present such papers—to present their ideas to their peers and receive feedback. This is certainly a perfectly good means of showing that a teacher has kept up with research.

If the goal of a college education is to develop an inquiring mind, how can we as teachers expect any less of ourselves than we do of our students? If we feel that students should be involved in research, that they should be pressing themselves to the limits of their own inquiry, then surely we should be doing the same as teachers. As graduation speakers often say, graduation from college is not an end to an education; it is the beginning. The sense of undergraduate education's being only the beginning should certainly be recognized by those who are going into college teaching. They should spend the rest of their lives deeply involved in their own education, so that they can be better teachers for those who come under their care.

That Grades Are Important

IN recent years there has been a return by politicians and educators alike to public statements about the importance of grades. These statements are often amplified by a call for stiffer grading of one sort or another. Almost no one says anything about doing away with grades any more, although that was the great cry during the 1960s. (I read an article the other day that claimed its purpose was to counteract the current mistaken praise for the educational practices of the 60s. What current praise? All I hear is misguided criticism of the decade. I had come to believe that I was the only one left who believed that it was one of the greatest periods of American education, second only to the influx of veterans after World War II.) I would like to argue that we were right in the 60s. In the first place, grades are always relative. At the present time, and as long as grade inflation remains with us, even the relative value of grades has disappeared.

In the late 1960s, I was in charge of the Liberal Studies Program at Elmira College. This program took the place of two full-time courses and covered a wide range of interdisciplinary material in a small-section, informal-meeting format. We decided that traditional grading would be done away with, and we would use just two symbols: S for satisfactory and U for unsatisfactory; but we would add written evaluations for each student. In order to avoid the problem of what to do with the equivalent of the D grade, we defined "unsatisfactory" as work below the norm, or traditional C, level. As one might predict, there was pressure almost from the very beginning that a third symbol be added in order to have a scale of honors, satisfactory, and unsatisfactory; and there were also faculty who wanted the further demarcation of high honors, honors, satisfactory, and unsatisfactory. Apparently no one wanted to fool around with the traditional D.

We stuck to our guns, and as I look back on the program, the grading or lack of it was one of the most successful elements. The reason is actually rather simple. Faculty members depend on grades almost as much as students do—perhaps even more. They are a crutch and a traditional crutch on which there is enough agreement to make the system work, even though it may be ultimately dishonest. (For example, why are an 89 and an 80 the same letter grade when 80 and 79 are different?) I would argue that grades are an unnecessary crutch. To shift the metaphor, if it is a carrot, it is the wrong carrot to offer when we are talking about a good education.

In my experience many of the very best students often get Cs. The reason is that they refuse to "learn the teacher" rather than the subject. There was an interesting phenomenon at Harvard during the late 50s and early 60s. Grades earned early in the semester suddenly began to be very high, and the Bureau of Study Counsel decided to find out what the cause of this shift was. They discovered to their great surprise that the students were not studying the subject as much as they were studying the teacher. They spent a good deal of time learning what the teacher wanted and giving it back to him. Unfortunately, by midterm that practice had led to a good many superficial responses.

Be that as it may, the main benefit of not using traditional grades is that it forces the teacher to make both good and bad comments on any paper handed back to a student. A grade makes it possible for a teacher to put into words only what is wrong with a paper, and a student deserves better than that.

In my own experience I have found that once I have given a student an A or a B, I assume the student knows that his or her paper is good. I then concentrate on what is wrong. But that is only part of what the student really needs. The student needs support as well as criticism. It is all very well to say that the conscientious teacher will make all the necessary comments, but I do not believe it works that way. Only when a teacher is forced to work without a grade is he also forced to make all the comments that should be given.

With the grade inflation that has taken place over the past decade, not only are the grades themselves misleading, but the students put an unnatural emphasis on high grades. At Midwestern, for example, there are many students who drop courses when they are getting Cs (when actually they should probably be getting Ds). This attachment to high grades for their own sake is debilitating, and it particularly hurts the best students.

When I started to teach, I felt that being a hard grader was important in some punitive sort of way. I found out very quickly that the real reason for grading hard was that it allowed the good students to know when they had really done a fine job. If everyone gets an A or B, there is no differentiation to let the better student know what he or she is doing.

Written comments are always more helpful for a good education than a grade at the top of a paper, and the more written comment, the better. (And written comments on course performance are a great deal more helpful for graduate schools and future employers than a mere grade!) This, it seems to me, was and remains the best reason for doing away with traditional grades.

But if grades are to be used, by all means let us pull them down to where they used to be and make C an institution's normal grade.

That Education Should Proceed from Simple to Complex Ideas

ONE of the more absurd ideas fostered in the teaching of teaching is that teachers should move their students from less complex to more complex ideas. In other words, start simple and then get complicated as you go along. According to this line of reasoning, one should never do anything very complicated in kindergarten, and really only by the time you reach high school should you be doing anything very hard. There is just one thing wrong with that idea: it flies in the face of everything that we know about the human mind. The mind is just as complex—indeed, it is much more complex—when it is young as when it is old. Somewhere around fourteen an entire process of generalizing takes place, and the number of synaptic connections drops by approximately one-half by the time one reaches twenty. That is one reason why it is easy to teach children foreign languages but much more difficult to teach them to adults. There are all sorts of things that ought to be taught to children that are currently held off until it is too late.

The point that I want to make is actually much simpler and is one that everyone really knows; yet almost no one pays any attention to it. I have certainly found no education program that pays attention to it. If I am wrong, I apologize to that program, wherever it may be, and on whichever planet it currently occurs.

When we have a young child under our tutelage, our own or someone else's, we go through a very "simple" teaching process. We take the child and point to an object outside the window and say "tree." Now the child is somehow or other supposed to make the connection between the sound "tree" and that object out there. The fact that what the child is looking at is an absolutely limitless, indeed almost infinite series of different shapes, all of different tones, not even all green, and yet is expected to equate every one of those individual objects, those unique experiences, with one generalized vowel sound with introductory consonant, "tree," is an incredibly complicated situation, and yet we think it simple.

Now, because we have a bright child on our hands, we say "tree" and we write on a piece of paper or on a blackboard "T R E E," and that child is now supposed to make the connection between the sound "tree" and those four hieroglyphs on the board or paper. It just so happens that in English the consonants and vowels for "tree" do have a somewhat clear relationship with the sound. The child is lucky that we are not using the word "tear" as our example, or "pear."

We now have a child who is supposed to make a connection between a sound "tree," an infinite number of objects in nature, of all shapes and sizes and conformations, and a connection between the four hieroglyphs and the sound "tree." We then expect him to make the connection between the four hieroglyphs and that infinite number of objects in nature on the assumption that two things equal to a third thing are equal to each other. Now just stop and think about it. There is no more complex learning situation that child will ever have to go through for the rest of his or her life. And yet, if the child can not make those connections immediately, we probably put him in a class of retarded children, or "slow learners." I repeat: there is no learning process more complicated that the child will have to go through, either as a child or as an adult. So why do we talk this nonsense about teaching children simple things so that they can move to more complex? They have already arrived at the more complex by the time they start.

There is a practical application to all this. As a matter of fact, there are several. You don't have to be John Stuart Mill or have a father like James Mill to realize that the ordinary human being is capable of so much more than he is currently achieving that as a culture we all stand under the criticism of robbing our young of their natural rights. The usual figure is that we use about 10 percent of our brain power. It makes little difference what the percentage actually is. The point is that we do not use most of our brains. Mill, whose I.Q. has been estimated (he lived before our more enlightened statistical age) at about 250, always claimed that he was an ordinary human being, with no better brain than anyone else. He may very well have been right. It was his father who believed that a child could and should learn. I certainly do not suggest that everyone should follow James Mill's theory of education. We would not have enough psychiatrists in the world to handle the results at the age of eighteen. Luckily John came out of his nervous breakdown through reading. But the point is that we can bring everyone up to a much higher level of education than he or she is currently achieving, and we can do so without much trouble. We are not, however, going to do it by the methods currently being taught by people in education programs. Nor are we going to do it by undervaluing students, I don't care what their backgrounds are.

What things do children need and what things do we know they can handle? We know, for example, that they can handle foreign languages with no problem whatever. Almost all of us have an example in our background of children and foreign languages. My favorite is a young boy out on the island of Mull, in western Scotland. I was cycling west toward Iona during the summer of 1949 and stopped off for a drink of water at a small farmhouse on one side of the road with a byre, or barn, on the other. A rheumatic, stooped old woman, who later I found was only thirty-five, came out and in a friendly fashion asked me in for tea. Her husband joined us, and soon their young boy, aged five, came in from the byre, where he had been mucking out after the cattle. As we talked, the boy moved, not only from sentence to sentence, or paragraph to paragraph, but from midsentence to midsentence from English into Gaelic and back, as he wanted to make sure that either I or his parents understood a point clearly. He was an ordinary Scottish farm child on a remote island, but his language ability was that of all children at an early age.

We hold up language training until we have to work with it as if it were a "foreign language," instead of a form of natural expression. Moreover, we often put teachers who have never become fluent in another language, who do not think in the language themselves but translate everything they say and therefore speak haltingly and without conviction, in charge of teaching children who can learn another language quickly and with no problem. America could be as multilingual as any other nation in the world simply by having languages taught from kindergarten onward, and taught well.

My second example is perhaps even more basic, and in the long run more important. Logic used to be part of the training of western man, and a necessary part. The ability to check the validity of an argument to see whether it stands any chance of being true is an absolutely basic need for human beings. In a democracy there is *no more* basic need. The ability to tell when a politician is speaking complete nonsense is one that any country, but especially a democracy, depends on. Logic is not taught very much anywhere any more, but it is certainly not taught at all—or even comprehended—in the lower grades.

The rules of logic—I speak now of traditional logic, not of symbolic, which can come later if it has to—are very clear. They are the kind of rules that can be made into a game. They do not need long periods of time to work on (there is no one more aware of attention-span problems than I am). But why are we not training our children how to think clearly? Why are we not giving them the rules with which they can check both themselves and others? It is certainly true that we are not; we are not even coming close to doing so. And I think there is a reason. I think it is one reason that our educational system is as poor as it is. We are afraid, both as parents and as teachers, when our children can check up on us; children who can show us our mistakes; children who have the tools to prove when we are wrong—and when they have a good argument.

As long as society does not want its children to be bright, we are going to have uneducated or poorly educated children. And the more we try to hide good thinking from our children so that we can defend ourselves against their attacks, the worse the educational system will be.

There is no question that the idea of working from simple to complex in educational terms is invalid. Until we stop thinking of it as valid, there will be nothing done to help education make the quantum leap of which it is capable.

R

That Tracking Is a Good Idea

IN the fall of 1968, I was asked to go to New College, in Sarasota, Florida, as provost (really Dean of the College). I flew down thinking that this was an excellent opportunity. I had already heard much about the college and its program of independent study. I had also heard about the quality of the students. At that point the average verbal SAT score was 692, a good deal higher than that at Harvard. On the first morning I was there, a very large part of the student body was sitting around the pool in the center of the new Pei campus. Strangely enough, almost no one was speaking to anyone else. These students appeared, instead, to be sitting around studying their own navels, intellectual or otherwise. The morale was obviously quite low in spite of the brilliance of the students who were there.

I had never really thought much about tracking before this experience. I had grown up in schools long before such systems had been put in effect, although it is true that we had some differentiation between college preparatory students and commercial students in our high school. At the same time there was considerable overlapping in the classes. But looking at that swimming pool and talking with the students, I suddenly realized that there was something basically wrong with tracking. It is true that a good education requires a student to play his mind off against other students; and the theory goes that the better the others are, the better the education will be. But in point of fact, the best minds need something else in their educations: they need the opportunity to lead. This means that there have to be others to follow, and I think it is probably also true that there are many students who need to follow in order to get a good education. The minute you split up these groups in separate tracks, you begin to hurt both groups. It goes without saying that the slower students are hurt by not seeing the quicker students at work. But it is equally true that the best students are harmed just as much by not being able to exercise educational or academic leadership.

When I went to Elmira College, I was put in charge of the Honors Program. As a result of some of the studies we did there, and also as a result of talking with directors of other honors programs at conferences like the ones at the University of Colorado, I discovered something that is paid far too little attention to in American education. When you take a program that has been designed for honors students and open it up to bright normal students, the latter do better than the honors students. Certainly in the Liberal Studies Program at Elmira we found that the normally bright students did far better in independent study than did the very bright ones. The reason seems to be that the average student realizes that he or she must put in a good deal of extra work to make the independent element come off. The very bright student tends to let it go, and therefore does not work either up to his or her own ability or even up to the ability of far less intelligent students. This same general situation held for the students who entered the early college program of Simon's Rock.

Mixed classes allow for better learning by everyone. They allow the better students to firm up the knowledge that they are getting by helping to teach or influence the less quick students, and they allow the slower students to work with the quicker minds, from whom they can also learn. It is probably true that wisdom is the seeing of the obvious. It has been my experience that slower students are very often able to see the obvious better than the bright students do. The average students may learn at a slower rate, but in the process they often see the basic core of an idea in a far better way than the brilliant students who pass over that core in favor of a superficial idea that attaches to it.

Tracking robs good students of many learning benefits. It harms poorer students by teaching failure and by leading them to have lower expectations of themselves and of the school system in general. In a democracy that depends on decisions made equally by all its members, tracking is a downright dangerous concept. No voting machine inquires what educational track the person pushing the lever was allowed to follow.

S

That Pornography Does Not Hurt the Reader or Viewer

THROUGH the years I have had to appear on a number of panels discussing the question of pornography and defending teachers from unwarranted attacks from churches, parents, and school groups for teaching good books, such as *The Catcher in the Rye*. I have even been put in the position of having to defend those who have been teaching not terribly good books. There is, however, a problem with all this, and I am the first to acknowledge it. It came to my attention in San Francisco, in 1962, when I was on a panel with members of the English Department of San Francisco State. After a number of us had said the usual things about why it is a bad thing to censor a book, Leonard Wolf spoke up. Leonard at that time was merely a good young poet, not the fine editor and critic of horror books like *Frankenstein* and *Dracula* he later became.

Leonard proclaimed to the audience that what was happening was dishonest, or if it wasn't dishonest, he was in the wrong profession. His point was a very good one. It was that what many of us had said sounded like the following: "Don't worry too much about pornography. Books aren't going to have all that much effect on your children's lives." Leonard's argument was that books have a lot of effect on people's lives, and if they don't, then we were in the wrong profession teaching literature. It is a point that was worth making then and still is.

Now let's shift the topic slightly. St. Paul writes, "Evil

communications corrupt good manners." At least that is what the King James translators give as the wording. The phrase is perfectly valid. Paul's point is that if you live in the presence of filth, your mind is going to get spotted. So is your behavior. I think of one particularly awkward set of incidents. I will not place them in any particular college framework. The story, however, is true. At one point, when sexual freedom was beginning to overwhelm college campuses (I don't mean books like *Candy,* but I do mean books like *Fanny Hill*), college nurses began to find observable physical problems among undergraduate women, as young people tried moving from innocence and virginity into full sexual practice—or extreme sexual practice—without anything in between. The damage was, in many cases, irreversible.

Now that is an extreme case. I am not at all suggesting that pornography inevitably or in any way necessarily leads to that kind of behavior. But pornography, no matter what its subject matter—or obscenity, and perhaps that is the better word, since to me wars are obscene—does corrupt good manners. It corrupts good thinking. John Milton was certainly a very brilliant man and one of my favorite human beings, and he wrote that evil can enter into the mind and not harm it as long as that evil is not accepted. It is a wonderful argument from *Areopagitica,* the greatest statement on freedom of the press in the English language. I have had cause to use it many times. It does, however, have a major flaw: it is not true.

Against John Milton I put any reader's experience. I do not believe that one can see a pornographic film (and I have seen all the classics in that genre) without being moved in one way or another. I know that one cannot view violence without being able to tolerate more violence the next time. This to me was the ultimate tragedy of the Vietnamese war. You cannot watch a Vietnamese officer shoot a prisoner in the head while you are eating supper and remain the same. Americans became used to violence, and they still are, and are becoming more used to it all the time. That is the reason that critics of violence on television are correct in their criticism. And that is the danger of the increasing emphasis on violence in the movies.

I am not arguing that one repeats what one sees or hears. I am simply arguing that one tolerates it more. And the more one tolerates such behavior, the less good there is in the world. If we tolerate it, then after a while we come not to care what other people do, at least what they do to themselves. But there is no way to stop that "to themselves" from moving "to others," and those "others" may indeed be ourselves.

Pornography, as becomes clear to those who have read very much, always moves in a particular direction. It starts in what we might call "fun" or pleasure (and with *Candy* never really leaves that stage), it moves toward lesbianism or homosexuality, and ends up in sadism or violence. It does corrupt good manners. It corrupts good lives. It diminishes the strength of moral judgments. It cuts down on quality judgments.

But this problem should not be seen merely as sexual. Where it is seen merely as sexual, the true issues are never really brought to light. It is always violence that is the true obscenity. Pornography, because it leads toward violence, is dangerous. It is dangerous to the individual; it is dangerous to society; it is dangerous to the world.

Unfortunately, most forms of censorship are even more dangerous.

T

That History Is What Happened

ALMOST everyone has some favorite quotation about history. Henry Ford's favorite dictum was "History is Bunk." Almost all students today know the line that he who does not know history is condemned to repeat it. I think my favorite criticism of history is that it is all passé.

During the 60s and the great controversy over relevance, history courses found themselves with few takers. History departments have not entirely recovered from the blows that that misguided concept of relevance struck against them. There certainly is a continuing distrust of the subject on the part of many—and not just among students. The idea that we should learn from history remains current, but no one is quite sure what that means. Although Solomon was right that there is nothing new under the sun, there is certainly nothing that ever repeats itself exactly either. Yet at the same time that there is distrust, there still is, as there always has been, something magnetic about the study of history. Sometimes it takes the form of the small-town antiquarian who makes records of local tombstones and church registers; sometimes it is the person who organizes and fights for the protection and refurbishing of older homes and buildings. Perhaps the most obvious form of the magnetism of history is seen in American tourists overseas, who almost without exception return filled with the desire and determination to read more history. The fact that they do not actually do so is no denial of the magnetism they felt at the time.

But the study of history can be misleading, and it can be very confusing, if we believe that history is what actually happened. All too often the subject is taught that way, especially in the lower grades. History is certainly not that. The reason is obvious: we do not know what happened. We don't even "know" what happens in our own lifetime. We can attempt to come to some kind of objective knowledge, but it is always just that: an attempt. Any courtroom trial provides evidence that history is not what happened. When witnesses to a specific event as traumatic as an automobile accident are unable to come up with a single agreed-upon set of information, it becomes obvious that any attempt to describe events in the past is not only impossible, but we are always at such a distance from the true facts that widely varying interpretations can quite honestly be drawn.

I suspect that scholars and publishers are to blame for much of the feeling that history is what happened. I remember, for example, submitting a manuscript to a university press of a biography of John Donne that I had originally written as a Ph.D. thesis. I had, in the process of writing the volume, inserted the words "probably" or "perhaps" quite often. The fact is that we just do not know many events in the life of Donne although we can guess at them. The editor said that he was interested in the book if I would eliminate all the "probablies" and "perhapses." This I refused to do. It made no sense to me to claim to know what Donne had done when I was not sure on the basis of historical records or manuscripts. The editor's reply was an interesting one. He said that the reader took for granted the tentative nature of historical evidence. I do not believe this is the case. I believe that readers, when they read straightforward statements of fact, believe what they read, or they at least believe that the authors mean them as facts. They do not constantly keep reminding themselves that this is only the writer's opinion. More recently I have had the experience of writing a biography of a man named John Hoskyns, who was a Member of Parliament in the seventeenth century. In the process I had to read all the standard works on late Elizabethan and Jacobean Parliaments. It was fascinating to me to note the generaliza-

tions that writers make about political "parties" at the time.
While I can see in the records of Parliament reasons for a
scholar to believe such parties existed, I can certainly find no
evidence in the records that they did, in fact, exist, or that we
can make any sure statements about them, at least without
strong qualifications. And if they did exist, it is impossible
for me to place Hoskyns, who was a leader in those sessions,
clearly in any one of them.

The recognition of the importance of history is certainly
essential in dealing with an educational institution. One is
always living with the history of that institution, or that
department, or that particular group of people. If one wants
to be effective in working with the institution, one has to
take into consideration that history. But it can sometimes be
dangerous to know too many of the facts. The reason is that
people are reacting to what they think happened, not to what
might actually have happened. If people think that an administrator has misused his power or made a decision on a selfish
or misguided basis, it is not usually worthwhile to act on the
basis that such was not the case. If those involved think that
the events should be read in a certain way, one had better pay
attention to their reactions rather than to information that
they do not believe.

Obviously there has to be some point in between what
people simply think happened and what actually happened.
We have to strive for all the objectivity we can muster. We
have to take into consideration as many "facts" as we can.
But we also have to realize that George Orwell, in *1984,* was
both right and wrong. He is clearly right in arguing that the
purposeful rewriting of history is one of the most dangerous
acts that men can do to each other. It can cut us off from our
own roots. It can teach us lies about human behavior. But it
is also true that, as we do not know what actually happened
in any situation in the past, we are constantly in the position
of having to rewrite history. By that I mean that we must
reinterpret the meaning of what has happened. For one thing,
we must keep our eyes open for any new evidence that would

bring us closer to the actual events of the past. But equally, we must seek to find out what people thought of those events and what their reactions can mean to us today. In other words, we must be in a constant process of reevaluation.

We all know some stories which we were told as children that we later on found were not true. Some, like George Washington and the cherry tree, were not crucial to our understanding of history. But our schools still teach as historical facts many stories that are extremely misleading. It is simply not true, for example, that everyone in Columbus' time thought the world was flat. Every educated person from at least the time of Dante in 1300 knew it was spherical. It had been described in that way in the *Divine Comedy,* one of the most influential volumes in the history of mankind. The popular views of Galileo dropping balls off the Leaning Tower of Pisa in order to discover the principle of gravity or watching the great lamp in the cathedral (which was not placed there for nearly a century after his death) in order to understand the principle of the pendulum are very misleading when used in teaching students to understand the principles of science and scientific investigation.

None of this means that history is any less important. As a matter of fact, it may mean that it is more important than we give it credit for being.

Long ago, as a child on a lake in New England, I discovered a metaphor that has given me an idea of how important history really is. I learned that when rowing a boat I had to set my bow correctly toward my goal, but from then on, I had to keep my eye fixed on a point behind the boat on the far shore in order to keep my course straight. It is clear that we must have clear goals toward which we work, but we had better keep our eyes fixed firmly on the past if we are going to be successful in achieving those goals. Otherwise we're liable to end up in the wrong cove or on a beach with "No trespassing" signs. Worse yet, we're liable to drift over the edge of a dam.

That Artists Are More Sensitive

WILLIAM Wordsworth once said that the poet was a man like any other men but that he was more sensitive. In my experience on college campuses working with creative artists, I have found that they are more sensitive indeed, but they are more sensitive to their own feelings, not necessarily to those of others. The attribute that makes them different is not their sensitivity but the fact that they have developed better techniques for communicating. Put another way: they have developed their own artistic vocabulary. Sometimes that vocabulary is much like that of the rest of us, as in the case of prose writers; sometimes it is slightly different, as in the case of poets and painters and sculptors; sometimes it is almost unattainable for most of us, as in the case of composers of serious music.

I should like to present as an example of some artists' lack of sensitivity a writer with whom I worked for several years. I looked forward to joining one department as its chairman largely because I looked forward to meeting this man. I had read his novels, and they showed a sensitivity and care that was quite remarkable. He was equally impressive in his treatment of both men and women, and he was perhaps more impressive in his treatment of teenagers. He even liked cats and dogs in a special way. When I arrived, I encountered a man who was about as insensitive to his colleagues as any teacher I had ever met. And as far as I could tell, he was pretty insensitive to both his wife and children as well.

Approximately three nights out of every week for the two years I worked closely with him, he was on the phone, trying to get me to fire another young man in the department with whom he disagreed. Each night he would bring up some new criticism, none of which would hold up in court or even in a faculty committee. For two years I fought him off. After I had left the college, I was talking with my writer friend (for we were and still are good friends) one day, and he said, "You know, so-and-so is a very fine fellow. I have worked with him on a committee for the past year, and he is one of the best people in the college." I reminded him of the three or four telephone calls a week in which he had tried to have the man fired. He simply shrugged his shoulders.

Unfortunately creative artists on college campuses are not only often insensitive to their colleagues, but they are often quite insensitive to their students as well. I remember a painter on another campus who seemed to get some kind of perverse joy out of slashing the inadequate work of some of his less talented students. Not only do some artists often flay the emotions of their students when the latter are attempting their own creative work in stories or poems or paintings, or pieces of pottery or sculpture; but creative artists are often the worst teachers in the misuse of students for their own needs, and I include sexual needs among them.

On college campuses in general they tend to be the most wrongheaded of all faculty members in dealing with college problems. Often this is the result of a quite understandable selfishness on their part. They wish to get on with their work, and the academic red tape and nonsense of the usual college situation infuriates them. At the same time, if they are going to work on a college campus, they should be willing to take part in the activities of that college. They often do not show such willingness.

Now obviously I am overgeneralizing. I have many creative artist friends who are very different from the examples or the generalizations I have just made. They are hard-working, politically honest, sensitive to others' needs like other sincere members of the faculty. I think the best example of this sort of person was Walter Van Tilburg Clark, who was head of the writing program at San Francisco State. But Walter was not only a fine example of the creative artist, he was also a bad example of what happens to the creative artist on a college campus. He simply stopped writing. He was willing to help any one at any time. Students knew that they could drop in at any hour of the day or night, at his office or at his home. Colleagues knew he would meet their classes if they had to be missing for any reason. Walter was always there, always gentle, always kind. And Walter stopped writing.

There is a problem, and it is a real problem, for the creative artist on a college campus, or at any occupation other than his or her art. Other activities do get in the way of creativity. That is not, however, an excuse for a lack of tact, a lack of sensitivity on the artists' part. We should be grateful to them for their creations, and we should be as helpful as we can in helping them to get on with their work, which brightens and enriches our lives. But at least on the personal level, we should never give in to them because we think that their judgments are more sensitive or more understanding about individuals or group situations. They are not. In that regard, we should pay just as much attention to them as we do to any other human being, but no more.

That Economics Is a Science

THE favorite indoor sport in many American colleges and universities these days, especially in Texas, seems to be to see how much reorganization can take place without totally altering the basic academic structure. The supposed purpose of all this is to cut down on the number of administrators on the assumption that the fewest possible number of people should report to any one person. This misguided concept of administration has been dragged in from American business at the very moment that businessmen are learning just the opposite from their Japanese counterparts. The usual result of the changes simply seems to be that more people are hired in the central administration in assistantship roles.

The way the game is played is to try to figure out which subjects or departments can be moved in with which other subjects and departments under one department or division chairman. In the usual plan, foreign languages and journalism go in with English, followed by philosophy or any other department with too few faculty members to fight back.

The subject that ought to be moved—and moved radically—is economics. Certainly that subject does not belong with the sciences or even close to the sciences. The sciences have been historically those subjects in which, once the data have been collected, a clear and inevitable result or conclusion can be achieved. They are, to put it another way, mathematical in the nature of their proof or their probability. This is obviously not the case with economics.

There are several possibilities worth considering. The first, of course, is history. Economists have a pretty good track record in describing why events in the past happened the way they did as a result of economic causes or influences. Marx and his followers have added a very satisfactory (if not necessarily true) dimension to the study of history in recognizing the importance of means of production in the development of cultures and in the change of a culture's aims and objectives. It is certainly in looking at the past that economists have been able to achieve their best results and their most helpful results.

The trouble with placing economists in history departments is that they are constantly trying to predict the future. Not many legitimate historians are still willing to go out on that particular limb. The next choice, therefore, is for economics to be placed in the same department with political science (which is, of course, another bastardized use of the term "science"). The evidence of at least the last decade or so would certainly support this placement. As one looks at the various schools of economists and economics, it becomes immediately apparent that decisions about what kind of economic action should be taken are determined not by the facts but by the individual political position of the economist. If he is a political conservative, then he makes a given set of decisions about what the facts indicate as to the proper future action. He will, of course, want to cut down on government spending and try to reduce the national debt at the cost of much human misery, which he will lament as "inevitable" or "unavoidable." The liberal economist will want to raise taxes in some cases, lower them in others, always with the attempt to place the burden more on the rich than on the middle class or poor. And he will see the necessity of increasing economic growth by adding more government intervention to the market place. These are basically political decisions, not economic ones, or they are economic ones only secondarily. It would, therefore, be an honest move to identify economics as part of political studies, rather than the other way around.

There are several departments in which economics should definitely *not* be placed. Philosophy, for example, is already having a hard enough time just surviving and keeping its skirts clean of theological, social, and pseudoscientific influences. Mathematics could perhaps survive the union if it could keep the economists limited to building models. But it is having enough trouble trying to keep computer freaks from destroying the concept of "elegance" that has always been the hallmark of genuine mathematical inquiry.

But economics really ought to be placed among the arts. I have no suggestion as to which art has the most in common with economics, but as most new reorganization plans lump all the arts together in a Fine Arts Division anyway, there would seem to be no basic problem. The reason for placing economics with the arts is obvious. In the first place, when two economists can look at the same set of facts and come up with perfectly good reasons for two diametrically opposed solutions, they certainly do not belong in the sciences. At the same time it is also clear that some economists seem to be better than others. It is not that they are more intelligent (heaven forfend that any one should raise that issue! Some of my best friends are economists); but they seem to be able to read the facts in a way that calls for action that does seem to have beneficial results. There is no connection with any particular school of economists in this matter, however. It is very much a matter of the individual economist on any individual day. It would seem, therefore, that intuition is the deciding factor as to who, at any given moment, is a good economist. But intuition belongs to the realm of the arts, not of the sciences, although great scientists have their days of flashes of intuition as well. Any subject that depends as clearly as economics does for its practical results on the intuitive thinking and feeling of the individual economist certainly belongs in the Division of Fine Arts.

That Guilt Is Wrong

I ONCE suggested to a group of church people that the appropriate response for a Christian who was not going to give away his wealth or fortune to the poor and needy was at least to feel guilty. A young and very up-to-date woman spoke up immediately and said that she felt that all guilt was wrong, and she would rather respond with joy to doing right. But it seems to me that guilt in response to wrong action—or even to inadequate action or no action at all when it is called for—is not only appropriate but absolutely necessary if any improvement is to take place. I am not talking, obviously, about repressed guilt, free-floating anxiety, or any of those other good Freudian terms.

One of the main problems with behavioral psychologists is that they sponsor the idea among themselves and their students that simply adopting positive behavior patterns is all that is necessary in human affairs. I do not believe this is true. It seems to me that there is the equal necessity for recognizing wrong behavior, whether it be on the part of one's self or someone else. Behaviorists spend a lot of time talking about positive reinforcement as the way to get people to act well. But there is wrong behavior, and it is not just, as the behaviorists would term it, inappropriate. It is wrong; sometimes it is downright evil. Positive reinforcement is not a satisfactory response to the presence of evil.

Herman Melville once said about the philosopher Ralph Waldo Emerson that the trouble with Emerson was that he had no room for evil in his cosmology. It is a fair criticism. I suspect that it is also the reason that millions of Americans read Herman Melville rather than Ralph Waldo Emerson. We admire authors who present us with a world that matches our own experience. The lesson of the holocaust—or of the elimination of the kulaks in Russia, or of the massacre of millions in Indonesia—is that there is evil action in the world, not just inappropriate acts.

Until people recognize their guilt, there seems to me no internal motivation for change. This is not a new idea. The lesson of Christianity throughout its history is that there is a necessary "conviction of sin" which must take place before repentance can follow. King David was equally aware of the positive and cleansing element of guilt in order for future action to follow.

America, during the quiz show scandals on early television, lived through the experience of watching a university faculty member, from a distinguished academic and literary family, Charles Van Doren, cheat on a quiz show and win vast amounts of money and a position with the broadcasting company. He pleaded with the Columbia faculty not to dismiss him. He said he was sorry, hoping, I suppose, that he would be positively reinforced by the faculty. Someone on the faculty pointed out that he had not given up the house, the car, or the money that he had gained from his cheating. He did not offer to do so at that point, either. The faculty, quite rightly, booted him out. There was no sense of wrongdoing on his part, but he undoubtedly thought his actions had been inappropriate, and he was undoubtedly sorry.

Now all of this does have at least one educational application that is worth noting. During the late 1960s a great many wooly-minded faculty members argued that faculty should not give failing grades to students (and at Brown, they still don't). Their argument usually entailed something like the following: if a student fails, it is the teacher's fault; or, it's not that the student really failed, it is simply that he or she did not succeed; or, it would be a terrible thing to label a student's action as failing on the college record that goes out to graduate schools, businesses, and so on.

Of course, the fact is that many students do not merely not succeed. They fail. Moreover, if they are going to change, they need the awareness of failure. If there is no sense of guilt involved, there is likely to be little positive change.

Every teacher at one time or another in his or her life receives a letter from a former student that makes the profession of teaching one of the, if not the most worthwhile and satisfying of professions. My favorite was a letter from a student whom I had flunked out of Middlebury College as a freshman. Not only had I flunked him, but I had flunked him on board a boat sailing to England, and I must admit that that bothered even *my* conscience. The student went into the Navy for a couple of years, then returned to Middlebury College to restart his education. The letter was written on the night before his graduation. He pointed out that he was not at the dance but was writing this letter instead. He wanted to thank me for failing him. He recognized that it might have been possible for him to continue his education had I not flunked him and to graduate in four years, but he would never have attained the education he did after he returned to college ready to do the work.

Guilt, of course, is not enough. By itself it accomplishes nothing. Change is needed: change to make up for the mistakes that were the causes of the guilt. But without the awareness of the wrong that was done, at least in my own experience and in the experience of those I have been able to observe through the years, no real change in behavior takes place.

X

That Equipment Makes a Difference in Learning

FOR the past two decades I have fought on every campus on which I have taught for a requirement in the introduction to the computer. I have done so for two main reasons: the first is that I do believe that education ought to have some relationship to the real world into which the student is going after graduation; the second, and more important to me, is that I want students to learn the limitations of the computer. The computer is a very stupid machine. It simply knows how to reply to questions with yes and no answers faster than human beings can. It is extremely useful in eliminating the drudgery and complexity of mathematical computation. But it is very little help in the process of thinking, no matter how much computer experts praise the new field of "artificial intelligence." I have been listening to the claims of these experts ever since the late 50s at Case Institute, and find the same fallacious thinking in their parallels between machine thinking and human thinking now that I did then. The most important difference is that the computer gives yes and no, black and white, answers, when most of the important questions in life call for more tentative and guarded answers.

There are similar drawbacks with teaching machines. Every study with which I am familiar indicates that once you get past the initial period of experimentation and are in a position to avoid the Hawthorne effect, there is not very much difference between students who have learned a subject on a teaching machine and those who have learned it in the classroom; little difference, that is, on quantitative measures. There still remains a great deal of difference on qualitative measures.

I once knew an education professor who tried very hard to convince me that I should put my courses in literature on to a teaching machine. He explained that a student could guess the right answer for a given question and then check to see whether it was right or not. I pointed out to him that there was nothing really very worthwhile that I could think of to put on a teaching machine for a course in Shakespeare. It is true that I could ask questions about the names of characters, the names of locations, dates, and so forth. None of these seem to me to be very important in the study of Shakespeare. I asked how, for example, one could place on the machine the question of why mankind has found *Hamlet* to be important to individual readers and, indeed, why it seems to mirror some universal experience. He suggested I make a list. I started a conversation with someone else.

My distrust of machinery in relation to education really began while I was teaching humanities to engineers at Case. It was in those days that engineering professors were beginning to discover that too great dependence on physical equipment in the teaching of engineers had strong negative effects. For one thing, it did not train the engineer for the future; it trained him for the past. They were beginning then to experiment with and come up with good courses utilizing theoretical and interdisciplinary approaches among the sciences.

The dangers in trusting too much on machines of any kind is obvious. For one thing, a power failure renders them absolutely unusable as a crutch to learning. For another, computers and calculators suffer from a characteristic similar to the problems surrounding the teaching of New Math, namely, that they do not help the student know what he is doing if he does not know the basic arithmetic procedures. It is still true, as it was at the beginning of the computer age, that the computer is as accurate as the operator. This can have cosmic consequences: consider the case of the lost Korean air liner over Russia.

But machines, especially machines with memories, are very much like book underlinings. They are valuable as a means of going back for information, but they are certainly not very useful in terms of thinking unless the material gets into the head. Machines that store information are like good reference books. It is, of course, a great help that such information can be gotten at easily. ("Retrieved" seems a strange word in computerese, as nothing has been lost.) And it is also a help that one does not have to memorize it all, such as the logarithm tables, for example. In this way, machines are very helpful indeed. But for thinking and learning, they are not: thinking and learning can only take place in the head.

It is therefore ironic that most schools and colleges are far more ready to expend huge sums of money for machines than they are for teachers, as if the purchase of a machine was going to solve all of the educational problems. Machines are, in the long run, more costly than human teachers, not less. One must continually keep up to date by purchasing new equipment, and the cost of maintaining complex machinery is staggering. But as long as school boards and boards of trustees keep looking for easy answers to educational problems that have no easy answers, we will probably find more and more machinery piling up in buildings around the country. Why is it, therefore, that when anyone talks about a really successful program of learning anywhere in the United States or around the world, we find that what is being described ultimately is a good teacher rather than a good machine?

That Vocational Education Is Good Practical Education

OVER the last decade there has been an increasing movement in colleges and universities across the country toward stressing vocational education. This movement has been fostered by a belief that colleges should be "practical," that they should prepare students for the "real world." There is nothing, of course, wrong with being practical. But I would submit that vocational education is neither practical nor the best way to prepare students for the real world.

Cardinal Newman said it best a century ago:

> . . . general culture of mind is the best aid to professional and scientific study, and educated men can do what illiterate cannot; and the man who has learned to think and to reason and to compare and to discriminate and to analyse, who has refined his taste, and formed his judgment, and sharpened his mental vision, will not indeed at once be a lawyer, or a pleader, or an orator, or a statesman, or a physician, or a good landlord, or a man of business, or a soldier, or an engineer, or a chemist, or a geologist, or an antiquarian, but he can take up any one of the sciences or callings I have referred to, or any other for which he has a taste or special talent, with an ease, a grace, a versatility, and a success, to which another is a stranger.

Of course, he had a clear idea of what he meant by a liberal education:

To open the mind, to correct it, to refine it, to enable it
to know, and to digest, master, rule, and use its knowledge, to give it power over its own faculties, application,
flexibility, method, critical exactness, sagacity, resource,
address, eloquent expression. . . .

Also in the middle of the nineteenth century, Ralph Waldo
Emerson stated that the goal of a good education was to train
"man thinking." What he meant was that we didn't train a
man to be a farmer, but a thinking man who farms. We often
forget how little of one's life is spent on the job. If we are
being "practical" about training for the real world of the
future, we should keep that in mind. Are we educating
people just for jobs or are we training them for life? Are we
educating people who will be "thinking persons" or are we
training people for the eight hours out of twenty-four that
they are at work? Actually, in the future it is likely that we
will be working less than that eight hours a day (and I am not
considering weekends, holidays, vacations, and so on).

But I am driving at something even more "practical" than
that. Back in the mid-1940s, while I was still an undergraduate, we made a survey of business, law, and medical schools
and asked them what they wanted in the way of graduates
from college; what kinds of majors did they want or look
for? Almost without exception, they answered that they
wanted liberal arts, or at least liberally educated, students.
The businessmen pointed out that most businesses do their
own training anyway. The medical schools said that they
wanted a liberally educated person who was a good, understanding human being as well as someone who could be
trained as a good doctor. They still say this, but I have to
admit that they do not often show it when making selections
of future students for medical school. Law schools still say it,
and they do mean it. I am always surprised by students who
talk about a "pre-law" major. I don't even know what that
really means. Most of the law students that I know who have
done extremely well in law school were those with tradi-

tional academic majors. Among my own former students, for example, I have had three editors of law reviews; all of them were English majors. Among the humanities majors I have had at Midwestern, a large percentage have gone on to and been successful at law schools. The clue to success in law school lies in the background in research that a student has obtained in college.

Businesses certainly should mean that they want well trained, liberally educated people. They have used some of the ideas from the liberal arts to make progress in their own businesses. In a sense, for example, "brainstorming," which at one time was such a popular phrase and which is still used but with less fanfare, was a product of liberal thinking, thinking freely. Many major companies send their executives off to summer programs and winter seminars at places like Williams and Amherst and Columbia, where the executives study Plato and Aristotle rather than business techniques. Of course, businesses want more than just liberally-educated persons. They want pushers; they want dynamic people. Business courses do not breed dynamic people. Neither, of course, do liberal arts courses. But if you have a dynamic person, the one who is trained to think freely is going to be the better person in business. At least once every two or three months a major newspaper or magazine carries an article or interview by a successful businessman who states that he chooses liberal arts majors for his company because they will think more freely and will be able to face the problems of the future more easily. Such articles usually stress the fact that the liberal arts major is more capable of doing the right kind of research as well.

I have always thought there is another idea that should be dispelled from the start in any discussion of this whole matter. When one talks with students, they often admit that the business courses they are taking are not very interesting or, in the long run, probably very helpful, but they say that the degree itself will get them the job they are looking for. Even if that is true, which I doubt—most of the businesses that have come to the colleges at which I have taught list "those with business or liberal arts training" as candidates for interviews—it is important to remember that a college degree counts exactly once in most people's careers. From that moment on, it is the quality of education that the student has had and the kind of performance the individual shows on the job that count.

There are many examples that could be given of the importance of being liberally educated in a vocational world. I have mentioned in an earlier essay that engineering schools discovered in the late 40s that it was important for engineering students to receive a good general education. The Hammond Report recommended that between a quarter and a third of an engineering student's education should be in the humanities and social sciences. The report was an important one and had a tremendous effect in the following decade. The conclusion that a good general education was important was based on the fact that over 50 percent of the students entering engineering schools changed their majors before they graduated. Having a strong general education background allowed them to make that change more easily. But even more important, the report revealed that five years out of engineering school, over 50 percent of the engineering graduates were no longer in engineering. Many of them were in management and executive roles. This, of course, did not mean that their engineering training was unimportant, but it did mean that equally important was the fact that such graduates needed a general education, a more liberal education that would help to prepare them to work with human beings at a more skillful and sensitive level than technical courses would train them for.

Another reason for the emphasis on general education training in technical schools was the recognition that the number of materials the engineers, for example, were having to work with was increasing daily, and that most of them had not even been in existence before the Second World War. Machines are constantly changing. There are constantly new problems, and new problems call for new solutions. New solutions call for a mental freedom to approach problems with a liberal mind.

Certainly problems we face in the future, problems of energy, problems of pollution, problems of ethics and values, which we are more and more faced with, these are problems that can best be solved by a large number of liberally educated people.

I would argue that a vocational education all too often narrows or closes a person's mind because it trains for the present. But any education that trains for the present is actually training for the past for the student once he has graduated from college. A liberal education keeps men's minds open; it trains them to think. Of course, I am not limiting the liberal arts to such traditional subjects as history or English or the classics. The sciences and mathematics are and always have been a major component of the liberal arts. The liberal arts should, indeed, be liberating. They should also train people how to communicate, and if there is any major problem from which we suffer in the world today, it is the problem of poor communication. Tom Lehrer once made the wonderful remark that all-too-succinctly states the issue: "I always thought that if a person said he couldn't communicate, the very least he could do is shut up."

Newman is right. It is still obviously true that a profession requires a liberal education. What is too often not recognized is that a good liberal education can make almost any job into a profession.

Z

That a Good Teacher Education Program Is Possible

MANY of the essays in this volume have raised the question either explicitly or implicitly of the necessity of teacher education programs or at least of education majors in colleges and universities in the United States. It is worth considering that question squarely and openly.

In all of the colleges at which I have taught across the country, there have been what I would consider three successful models for teacher education programs. One of them, at Middlebury College back in the 40s, was a rather simple setup in which one member of the faculty offered a handful of courses and supervised the practice teaching of seniors who wished to gain a teaching credential upon graduating. All of the students took regular academic majors in the college and fulfilled the same general academic program that the other students at the college did. The education courses were taken as electives on the side. It must be stated, however, that student response to the education courses was as noncommittal or negative as it was in all the other programs I am aware of. It is just that no one felt that his or her education was hampered by those courses.

In the 50s and early 60s, a group of education programs known familiarly as MAT programs (Master of Arts in Teaching) gained widespread popularity. In general, the program ran as a followup on a traditional undergraduate program with an academic major or major and minor. The usual pattern was that students would complete their BA or BS at a liberal arts college, then move to a School of Education such as that at Harvard, at which they would take courses beginning in the summer following graduation and running through the following academic year. During that year the student concentrated on teaching and education courses, although in most of the programs with which I was familiar, there was also some very strong advanced work in the subject matter area as well. During the initial summer session, the students often observed courses taught by Master Teachers; sometimes there was actual teaching involved at this point. During the fall, both academic and education courses were taken. The crowning point of the program was, of course, the teaching experience in the spring semester of the regular academic year. There is no question that the MAT program worked, but there was unfortunately an inescapable reason for such programs to be dropped at university after university. It was simply too expensive to run. There was no long-term way for the universities to support that cost.

The third model was that which we managed to push through in California in the early 60s. We required that every student intending to go into teaching had to fulfill a regular major in an academic field first. That included students who were planning to go into teaching at any level, from kindergarten on. In general it meant that satisfying major requirements pushed the teacher candidates into a fifth year. That was not necessary, but it was certainly the usual result. The methods courses were all taught within the subject matter departments.

These three programs had some very important similarities. The first, of course, was that each student had to complete a regular major in a discipline or subject matter area before he or she was allowed to go on to the credentialing program. There was no manufacturing of weakened requirements either in the traditional major or in the general education requirements of the university for those who were going into teaching. The second, because of the first, was that the student had basically completed the major before taking any education courses. In other words, a student had the basic knowledge of the subject matter in the field that he or she was going to teach before undergoing courses in the teaching of that subject matter. This was, of course, particularly true of the programs that took place in the fifth year of a student's university education. The third was that teaching methods were primarily taught by faculty in the subject matter area.

Discussions about training and credentialing of students who are to teach in elementary or high schools often leave out an extremely important point. School systems act as if it were really necessary for a prospective teacher to have gone through a teacher education course. As a matter of fact, some of the very best teachers in many of the best private schools in the United States have never had any education courses, and they certainly never intend to have any. Equally important, most school systems have a way of allowing a good prospective teacher to get into the process and *then* satisfy state requirements for the credential by taking teacher education courses after they have already begun to teach. That strikes me as being a bit illogical, although I am happy that the loophole is there. What it really means, of course, is that the education courses are not necessary for good teaching. They are a requirement added after the fact.

There is really no way for us to discover what the practical effect of doing away with teacher education requirements might be as long as the state agencies empowered with governing education requirements in the states are run by educationists. What is needed is a concerted experiment in schools across the country using prospective teachers who have not gone through any education program but who have shown their ability as students in the fields they are going to teach. Unfortunately, the examples that come most quickly to mind and that indicate that such experimentation will never take place are those that are the most depressing. In Texas during the last few years there have been a number of movements to do something about the poor quality of teaching. One of those movements was the giving of examinations in subject matter competency to teachers in various city systems. In a frighteningly large number of cases, the teachers could not pass the examinations—which were *extremely* simple. Members of the state legislature, feeling quite rightly that they should do something about the situation, asked the state board and the state education agency to examine what could be done. The various education agencies gathered together, mobilized partly by the departments of education of the universities within the state, and came up with a recommendation that is incredible to me. They suggested that *more* time be spent in education courses rather than less, and less time be spent in the subject matter areas rather than more. In an early stage of their recommendations, they even suggested that education departments should state the requirements of the subject matter majors for prospective teachers. This flies in the face of every single piece of evidence that any of us have about the nature of the best training for prospective teachers.

A couple of years ago I was acting as a consultant to a small college in Ohio at the time that the state board made its recommendations for improvement in teacher training. They were just as ruinous as the ones I have just described. The recommendations I saw then would require prospective teachers to be involved in class observation of one kind or another across almost the entire four year period of undergraduate education. This meant that the students would effectively be kept from getting a decent education of their own. They would be being taught how to teach before, and in place of, their getting any knowledge of subject matter to teach. They would, presumably, then transfer their weakened personal education on to their students.

What do we really need for prospective teachers that all of us could basically agree on? I think that the answer turns out to be a remarkably small list of courses. First, any student who wants to be a teacher probably ought to take a course or two in child and adolescent psychology. But these courses should not be taught in an education department; they should be taught by faculty in the psychology department. Second, it may be true that methods courses in subject matter areas should be taught to prospective teachers, but, if that is the case, then two further points should be made immediately. First, the methods courses should not be offered until after the student has already gained knowledge of the material at hand; and second, those methods courses should be taught by faculty in the subject matter area. If a further requirement is necessary, that such faculty should themselves have had experience in teaching in primary or secondary schools, then so be it. I am sorry, but as I have said earlier, there is very little that can be said intelligently about teaching methods in general, but there are things that can be said about specific methods in subject areas. It takes someone who knows the subject area to talk about the methods with intelligence, however. Third, certainly the one requirement for anyone going into public school teaching should be practice teaching. But again, practice teaching should be supervised by people in the subject area. Actually the best plan for practice teaching, and I have seen it work in several colleges, is for the college to enlist the support of those teachers who are named Master Teachers and trust in the judgment of those master teachers for the comments and criticism of the student teacher. Such teachers can be given adjunct faculty positions on the college faculty so that they can give grades.

I suspect that there may be one other possible requirement, and that is in elementary education. It is probably true that someone going into elementary education should spend a semester before practice teaching observing a good elementary teacher at work. There are special problems at the elementary level, and it would be foolish not to admit it.

But we all really know what is needed in the training of good teachers. What is needed is a good, strong general education with courses that require hard work and real knowledge on the part of future teachers. It requires a full academic major for the student in the field which he or she is going to teach at any level in the schools. I have seen too many prospective primary teacher candidates receiving help in "getting through" mathematics requirements, for example, when everyone involved, including the student, admitted that he or she really didn't understand mathematics. I certainly would not want any of my children to have such a teacher. I still think that we were right in California that even elementary school teachers should be forced to carry a full academic major even though the elementary teacher is going to teach a number of different subjects. A teacher ought to know how to go about gaining firsthand knowledge of a subject, how to do the research, how to use the library facilities. The only effective way I know to do that is to force a student to considerable depth in a program of academic study. The elementary school teacher needs that training just as much as the secondary school teacher does. I suppose one requirement that could be added is that the elementary school teacher might well be urged to take both a strong academic major and a strong academic minor as well; and the two that come immediately to mind would be English and mathematics.

All of this may seem to imply that college teachers in academic subjects are "hotshots" in general. I have taught too many places with too many people to believe that is true. I am perfectly aware of the dangers of the usual academic major. I am thinking particularly of the fact that so many faculty within majors now communicate in a jargon or bastard English that is almost impenetrable, and I do not except the English departments of the country from that criticism. Over the past twenty years as I have been writing reviews for *Choice,* the library journal, I have become more and more depressed by the low level of the prose written by people who are obviously teaching English courses in colleges and universities. That, however, does not mean that stressing an academic major is wrong; it simply means that colleges and universities should be riding their faculties hard for proper teaching and written expression in their courses.

There is no substitute for learning the subject that one is going to teach. All the education courses in the world will not take the place of that experience, and even the best education courses will not give a prospective teacher the training that he or she needs to communicate subject matter to future students.